PRAISE FOR THE BOOK

D1295352

"A marvelous mélange of suggestions for storybooks to read, crafts ac_____ delicious cookery projects, all to be enjoyed together by parent and child. The book is clearly grounded in a good understanding of kids' feelings and fears, dreams and developmental stages. In six thematically grouped chapters, Kirkfield ties each read-aloud book to a related crafts activity and cooking activity, each of these fulfilling a purpose and/or delivering an important message for all pre-school-age kids and helping them feel positive about themselves. A valuable resource for parents!" **Cynthia MacGregor, Author of Stranger Danger, Divorce Helpbook for Kids, and over 50 other books**

"As a physician and parent, I find this book to be an exceptional guide for mothers and fathers who want to have fun teaching their children as they grow. Parents and children stand to learn a lot from each lesson, and the bonding created through cooking and crafts will make learning fun for all involved." **Dr. Peter Clothier, Family Physician, Colorado**

"Kirkfield's first book of her new Positive Parental Participation series provides a way for parents and children to engage in a cooperative learning experience. A parent's participation and encouragement directly affects the child's attitude toward self-esteem, and SHOW ME HOW! is full of delightful, educational, and family-oriented activities that address each developmental milestone. SHOW ME HOW! is a framework of carefully crafted, multi-sensory lessons especially geared towards early childhood. This well-planned learning tool will promote a willingness to try new experiences and connect the child's knowledge and skills to a new personal level of mastery and unique sense of self." **Peggy Hicks, M.A. Special Education Teacher Pikes Peak Boces, Colorado Springs, CO**

"As both a clinical psychologist and a mother of two young children, I am certain that this book will be an incredible resource for families wishing to foster their children's sense of self-worth. Parenting is a difficult and complex task, and SHOW ME HOW! BUILD YOUR CHILD'S SELF-ESTEEM THROUGH READING, CRAFTING AND COOKING offers a road map through which parents can help their children feel valued, accepted and loved. Ms. Kirkfield presents concrete exercises and helpful recommendations that are sure to give parents a newfound sense of competence and confidence in their own abilities as well. This book will be an invaluable tool for parents, teachers, child-care providers, and anyone who is dedicated to the healthy growth and development of our children." **Jodi Harap, Ph.D., Licensed Clinical Psychologist and Mother of Two**

"Vivian Kirkfield's SHOW ME HOW! offers parents, grandparents, daycare providers, preschool teachers, and anyone else who works and plays with young children, a treasure trove of eco-friendly activities and easy and nutritious recipes based around a collection of 100 picture books that includes many old favorites as well as newer titles, too. Readers will benefit from her experience and wise counsel in her introductions to each chapter and her notes about "positive parental participation." Using this book with children will not only help build their self-esteem, it'll also turn them into life-long readers and lovers of books! I wish SHOW ME HOW! had existed when my own children were young." **Suzanne Williams, Author of over 27 children's books including the Princess Power and Fairy Blossoms series**

"Using many of the classics in early childhood literature and blending the stories with the hands-on experiences of creative crafts and cooking, the program peaks a child's interest and desire to learn. SHOW ME HOW! offers all of us a great tool to help our children become people of kindness, people open and well-rounded and people who are successful...for themselves and with others." **Mary Newquist, Assistant Principal, Our Lady of Perpetual Help Catholic School, Selma, TX**

"SHOW ME HOW! sure does show how! The parent or teacher who uses this book with young children will never lack for activities and projects!" **Joe Lasker, Author and illustrator of The Do-Something Day**

"Bright, fun and right-on-the-mark, Kirkfield's SHOW ME HOW! is an engaging book for parents, educators and child care facilitators who share a commitment in providing children with a wonder-filled day of activity. It's all here—story time recommendations, crafting exercises and cooking plans for little hands—I can't wait for her next book!" **B. G. Zajac, B.A., Former educator and child care facilitator, Omaha, Nebraska**

"Kirkfield provides the childcare world with a phenomenally creative book which contains a perfect blend of crafts, recipes and story recommendations for the daily challenges that confront our young children today. The message of building a child's self-esteem and confidence is present in each chapter. This book is A MUST AND SHOULD BE FOUND ON THE COFFEE TABLE in every parent, grandparent or child educator's home around the world!" **Jane Aquilone, Grandmother of 5 and former Youth Advisor & Drama Director, New Jersey**

"Show Me How" is a wonderfully creative resource for every adult who loves to spend time with young children. This book is full of insights and practical wisdom about the magical process of developing self esteem in young children. The stories and craft and cooking projects are aimed at helping children develop a sense of competency and recognize their exciting and sometimes overwhelming new world of feelings. This book is both a tool and a workbook that helps loving adults encourage children to identity their feelings, safely communicate their feelings appropriately, cope with stress, develop skills to problem solve, learn from mistakes, take responsibility for behavior, make healthy choices, and trust their feelings as they continue to mature and take on new challenges and life experiences." **Ellen Levy, MSW, LCSW, Executive Director, Adoption Choice Center, Colorado Springs, CO**

"With many years of innovative experience as a teacher, daycare provider and mother of three, Kirkfield lays out a brilliant and simple program to create balance and harmony for the entire family. Reading the picture book stories aloud and participating in the eco-friendly craft project and child-friendly cooking activity will inspire parents to develop their children's pre-literacy skills while forging a life-long bond" **Diana Loomans, Best-selling author of The Lovables in the Kingdom of Self-Esteem; What All Children Want Their Parents to Know; and 6 additional books**

"In working with parents of young children who feel the challenges that everyday life hands them, I appreciate the fact that Kirkfield's SHOW ME HOW! delivers what it promises: a fresh take on clear, concise learning plans that anyone can use. You don't have to be a rocket scientist to know that children need our time and attention. The productive activities that Kirkfield introduces create an atmosphere of caring and sharing and satisfy that basic need. It's a given: this is a winning book!" **Richard Zajac, M.S., Former lead facilitator: "Positive Parenting for Families", Family Services, Inc., Omaha, NE**

"SHOW ME HOW! is an invaluable resource book for teachers and parents. Congratulations on a well-researched, organized, easy-to-follow book with fresh new ideas! I'm looking forward to using it." **Marilee Gruber, Kindergarten teacher and grandmother of 5, Colorado Springs, CO**

SHOW ME HOW!

BUILD YOUR CHILD'S SELF-ESTEEM THROUGH READING, CRAFTING AND COOKING

Vivian Kirkfield

MoneyPenny Press, Ltd.
Colorado Springs, CO

Happy Reading, Crafting
+ Cooking!
Are the best.
Vivian Kirkfield

Copyright © 2010 by Vivian Kirkfield
First Edition

No part of this book may be used or reproduced in any manner whatsoever without written permission, except in the case of brief quotations embodied in critical articles and reviews. For more information e-mail all inquiries to: info@positiveparentalparticipation.com.

Published by MoneyPenny Press Ltd.
P.O. Box 26583
Colorado Springs, CO 80936-6583

ISBN: 978-0-9670147-5-3

Library of Congress Control Number: 2010925603

Cover and interior illustrations by Andrea Kirkfield
Interior layout and editing by Caroline Nigen

Contact Vivian Kirkfield at: vivian@positiveparentalparticipation.com

Printed in the United States of America

THIS BOOK IS DEDICATED TO:

My children: who are bright, loving, independent, creative, responsible adults. Thank you for teaching me more about parenting than any course I ever took or book I ever read.

My husband: who has been the love of my life for over forty years. Thank you for encouraging me to write this book and for being there for me every step of the way.

My mother: who read me my first picture book.
Thank you for instilling in me a love of reading.

My grandmother: who was a role model for Positive Parental Participation in an era before spending "quality" time with young children was considered crucial to building self-esteem. Thank you for giving me your unconditional love.

THERE ARE MANY OTHERS WHO NEED TO BE ACKNOWLEDGED:

The writers and illustrators whose talent and insight created beautiful picture books that are enjoyed by millions of children...

My friends and family who have been so supportive throughout this book journey...

My sister, who was willing to proofread the entire manuscript several times, not only for typographical errors, but also for recipe and craft logic...

And the many children whose lives I touched...hopefully that contact enriched their lives as they most assuredly enriched mine.

IN MEMORIAM:

Lucille Clifton (June 27, 1936 - February 13, 2010)
American poet, writer, educator and author of *One of the Problems of Everett Anderson.* She was a voice for children who had no one else to speak for them.

DISCLAIMER

The content of this book is intended for educational purposes only and does not constitute medical or healthcare advice or diagnosis. Please consult your doctor or other appropriate healthcare professional with any questions you may have concerning a medical condition.

The cooking and crafting projects suggested in this book should be supervised by a responsible adult. In addition, all activities recommended (for example: reading, crafting, cooking, etc.) should be adjusted accordingly for each individual child's abilities and maturity.
Every effort has been made to make this guide as accurate as possible, but there may be mistakes, both typographical and in content. The author, publisher and others involved in creating this book shall have neither liability nor responsibility to any person or entity with respect to any loss or damage caused, or alleged to have been caused, directly or indirectly, by the information contained in this book. The reader is ultimately responsible for the thoughtful and careful implementation of any ideas presented in this book.

The author, publisher, and their officers, directors, affiliates, successors, assigns, insurers, principals, agents, contractors, representatives, employees and attorneys involved in creating this book disclaim any and all liability for any and all claims resulting from or in any way arising or growing out of, and by reason of any and all known and unknown, foreseen and unforeseen claims, and the consequences thereof, regarding any liability arising out of the reader's use, interpretation, or implementation of any and all activities recommended in this book, including, without limitation, any actions regarding personal injury or property damage and including any such claims which allege negligent acts or omissions of the author, publisher, and/or their officers, directors, affiliates, successors, assigns, insurers, principals, agents, contractors, representatives, employees and attorneys involved in creating this book.

Any concepts, notions, ideas, suggestions and recommendations from this book that the reader accepts and/or applies to his or her life, the reader does of his or her own free will. Each reader bears sole responsibility for his or her own safety and well-being.

BRIEF TABLE OF CONTENTS

A Poem

If I Had My Child To Raise Over Again

"If I had my child to raise over again,

I'd finger paint more, and point the finger less.

I'd do less correcting and more connecting.

I'd take my eyes off my watch and watch with my eyes.

I would care to know less and know to care more.

I'd take more hikes and fly more kites.

I'd stop playing serious and seriously play.

I'd run through more fields and gaze at more stars.

I'd do more hugging and less tugging.

I would be firm less often and affirm much more.

I'd build self-esteem first, and the house later.

I'd teach less about the love of power,

And more about the power of love."

Diana Loomans © 2009

For more information on Diana's written works, visit www.dianaloomans.com

Table of Contents:

CHAPTER THREE: "I LOVE YOU AND YOU LOVE ME!"
How to help your children feel appreciated, loved and accepted…75

CHAPTER FOUR: "I AM REALLY MAD RIGHT NOW!"
How to help your children express their feelings…113

CHAPTER FIVE: "I'M AFRAID!"

How to help your children acknowledge and cope with their fears…145

CHAPTER SIX: "I LIKE MYSELF!"
How to help your children feel good about their bodies and themselves…181

INTRODUCTION

ONE PICTURE (BOOK) IS WORTH A THOUSAND WORDS
How picture books can help you solve problems with your children

Returning home from the hospital after giving birth to our second son, I stepped out of the car, holding our new baby in my arms. I approached the doorway where three-and-a-half year-old Jason was waiting to greet us. "Hi honey," I said. "Mommy's home! I missed you so much." With his eyes welling up with tears and his face a mask of emotions, Jason ran into the house yelling, "If you love me, why do you need him?" Taking a deep, calming breath, I went inside and quickly put the baby into the crib that had once been Jason's. Grabbing a copy of ***Peter's Chair*** by Ezra Jack Keats, I found Jason sitting on the floor in his room and knelt down beside him, holding out my arms for him to sit on my lap. His tense little body conveyed the fear and anger he was feeling. "No matter how many children I have, I will always have more than enough love for each one of you," I explained. Hugging him, I continued, "Let's read a story about another boy who also had a new baby in his family." The story unfolded as we turned the pages and Jason slowly relaxed, turning to me with a tentative smile, saying, "I missed you, too, Mommy."

After the story was finished, Jason's father helped him put up a new bulletin board that would display Jason's artwork. Later in the day, Jason joined me in the kitchen, where he helped me prepare peanut butter cookies, his favorite dessert. When he got ready for bed that night and we asked him to help us sing a lullaby to his new baby brother, Jason was eager to join in, sure in the knowledge that he had not been displaced by this new person, but was still a very important and special member of our family.

Helping your child develop a positive self-image is one of your primary goals (probably second only to food and shelter in importance) and this book is a unique tool that will enable every parent to meet that goal. Through my many years of involvement in the care and education of young children, I discovered the power of picture books and learned to use them, not only for entertainment and enjoyment, but also to help children deal with the various issues that they encounter in their formative years. During my tenure as a kindergarten teacher and day-care provider, I formulated a program that paired a particular picture book story with both an appropriate craft project and a cooking experience. I found that in using this process, **the children in my care were happy, loving, enthusiastic, independent, curious about their world, and eager to face new challenges...in effect, they were children with a positive self-image!**

Each of the six chapters of this book consists of fifteen or more picture book story suggestions, with summaries and commentaries for each book. There is also an appropriately matched arts and crafts project, in addition to a cooking activity, for each story. The books I have chosen for this guide address six elements that are crucial for building positive self-esteem: mastering tasks and skills, valuing one's strengths and qualities, feeling appreciated, loved and accepted, being able to express one's feelings, coping with and overcoming one's fears, and finally, accepting and liking oneself. **Each environmentally friendly arts and crafts project is geared toward recycling items already on hand** (such as old magazines and cardboard juice containers) so as to decrease the unbelievably large amount of garbage each family usually generates, while at the same time allowing your child to master skills and gain a sense of pride and accomplishment with his creation. In addition, you can use the recipes at the end of the book to make homemade paints and clay to avoid the harmful chemicals added to most store bought products. If you do buy your art supplies, please make sure that they are *non-toxic* and as "earth-friendly" as possible.

The cooking experience is also crucial because with each recipe the child helps to prepare, he gains confidence and competence and his sense of self-worth grows. The healthful natural recipes for snacks and meals include low fat, low sugar and high-fiber combinations to help increase mental and physical vitality. Substitutions can almost always be made to tailor the recipe to your family's needs; I use soymilk instead of cow's milk, an egg substitute instead of real eggs, Celtic sea salt instead of the store brand table salt. Because of the recent studies concerning margarine, you may want to substitute a more healthy non-hydrogenated spread. **The recipes don't specifically call for ingredients that are organic, locally grown and in season. However, using such ingredients will add immense health benefits to your entire family while creating a less damaging impact on the earth.**

I encourage all parents to take some time to look through the different chapters before using this book with your children. When you find the stories and activities you want to use, make a list of what you'll need (the picture book, craft supplies, ingredients and utensils, etc.) and check to see what you have on hand and what you will need to obtain. It's no fun to stop in the middle of a project because you can't find the paste, or to postpone making the promised treat because you are lacking one of the ingredients. Most of the books are available for loan at public libraries and many of the craft supplies are free (wallpaper sample books, old magazines and empty shoe boxes, for example) or are very inexpensive. You'll probably have many of the ingredients and utensils for the cooking activities in your kitchen already, but do check to be sure.

Another important suggestion has to do with the actual reading of the picture book story. Please make sure that you and your child are comfortable (perhaps sharing a space on the couch or sitting in a rocking chair with your child on your lap) and your child can see the pictures in the book without a strain. Reading to your child on a daily basis helps build pre-literacy skills. **I encourage you to set aside the time for this interaction with your child to make it special. This is not a time for multi-tasking, as proficient as we parents may have become at that!**

The last word of advice pertains to the age-appropriateness of the stories and activities. Although all are geared towards children ages two through five, each child is an individual in his own right. **You know your child better than anyone and can make modifications to any of the stories and activities when necessary.** The last thing that we want to do is to create an atmosphere of failure and frustration. All of the activities are appropriate for boys and girls, regardless of whether the text says "he" or "she" and "him" or "her". **Please also exercise caution during the cooking experience**…young ones should be pouring and mixing the ingredients in the bowls, not stirring the pot at the stove. Any cutting with sharp knives needs to be done by the parent or other responsible adults. In addition, please remember to wash hands before beginning the cooking project, any time hands have touched raw meat or poultry, and whenever you feel it is needed.

I believe that the "secret" ingredient for success with this program is <u>Positive Parental Participation</u>. When a parent takes the time to read a story to his young child, that child feels valued and loved and will be able to value and love others. When a parent listens without judgment to what his young child has to say, that child knows that she is important and will be able to respect what others have to say. When a parent participates joyfully in activities with her young child, whether collecting leaves on a nature walk, baking oatmeal-raisin cookies, singing a song or painting a picture, that child gains a sense of competence and self-confidence that will help him for the rest of his life. And that is what this book is all about!

NOTES:

CHAPTER ONE: I CAN DO IT MYSELF!

How to help your child master skills and tasks

Two-dozen hard-boiled eggs were cooling on the counter and three bowls of deeply colored water waited on the table. The children in my day-care group took their seats, eager to begin coloring and decorating Easter eggs. Setting an egg in an egg holder for each child, I handed out Q-tips and let the children draw their own designs with the colored water. After each child had decorated a few eggs, we let them dry so that they could be put into the baskets that the children had made the day before. As the children left the table, three-year old Stephanie bumped into four-year old Ben who was carrying a small bowl of unused eggs. CRASH! SPLAT! Down went the bowl! Away rolled the eggs! Both Ben and Stephanie sat on the floor, looking ready to cry. "Sorry," they both said at the same time. "Don't worry," I reassured them. "Let's pick up those eggs and throw them away because they are cracked. I know we are all happy that they are not the ones we decorated." As we cleaned up the mess, I added, "I have a special story to read to you about a little rabbit who decorated Easter eggs. One day he dropped some of them that weren't even cooked yet." Ben giggled, "What a mess!" "Yes, it certainly was," I replied, as we all went over to the story corner to read *The Chocolate Rabbit* by Maria Claret. Later in the day, the children joined me in preparing chocolate-dipped fruit.

> *"Nothing builds self-esteem and self-confidence like accomplishment."*
> *Thomas Carlyle*

POSITIVE PARENTAL PARTICIPATION NOTE:

Young children benefit from tasks and activities that offer a real challenge because their successes help to build a strong, positive self-image. They also need to hear about others who have faced obstacles and dealt with failure. By participating with your child in the activities in this chapter, you can help his self-esteem grow.

READING:
THE CHOCOLATE RABBIT

Written by Maria Claret
Translated by Joy Backhouse
Revised by Jane O'Sullivan
(New York: Barron's Educational Series, Inc., 1985)

Bertie Rabbit and his sisters want to help their artistic father who paints beautiful Easter eggs, but they are too young. One day, Bertie decides that he is old enough to help his father so he buys fresh eggs with his own money and carries them home in a basket. However, when he stops to pick flowers to decorate the basket, he trips and falls and the eggs tumble out of the basket and break. Bertie is very sad because he has failed to help his father. His mother makes a pot of chocolate the next morning to lift Bertie's spirits. Bertie smells the chocolate and climbs onto a stool so that he can get a tiny taste of the chocolate. Unfortunately, the stool becomes unbalanced and he falls off with the pot of cooled chocolate spilling all over him. Bertie's father sees his son covered in chocolate and has a wonderful idea to make chocolate in the shape of a rabbit. Everyone is very proud of Bertie because he inspired the making of the first chocolate rabbit and Bertie is proud of himself because he has reached his goal of helping his father.

POSITIVE PARENTAL PARTICIPATION NOTE:

Although we don't want to encourage young children to stand on stools to reach into pots of hot chocolate, we do want to encourage them to set goals and reach them. Bertie was willing to spend his own money to help his father in the family business and he was eager to take on more responsibilities as he grew up. The reaction of his parents when he experienced failure was quite positive, and this reaction helped Bertie to keep trying to master different tasks. By responding to our children's failures in a like manner, we encourage them to try, try again.

CRAFTING:
PAINTING EASTER EGGS WITH NATURAL DYES

You will need: Hard-boiled eggs (cooled), Q-tips, one or more of the following: ¼ cup blueberries (blue), ¼ cup cranberries (red), 1 tsp turmeric (yellow), markers, a small bowl for each color, cover-ups, two small pots, and water to boil.

1. Cover the work surface and workers to protect from staining.
2. Boil ½ cup water, add crushed blueberries, simmer for 5 minutes and then pour into a small bowl and let cool for a few minutes. Do the same for the cranberries.
3. Pour 1 tsp turmeric and ½ cup of hot water in a small bowl, stir and let cool.
4. Put an egg into each bowl and let sit for 5-10 minutes, turning several times with a spoon, then lift each egg out and let dry. Use markers to add designs.

COOKING:
CHILD-FRIENDLY CHOCOLATE-COVERED BANANAS

Tastes just like a banana ice cream bon bon!

You will need: 1 tsp margarine, ¼ cup evaporated milk, 2 oz dark chocolate (in pieces), 1 banana, a pot, a cookie sheet lined with wax paper, and toothpicks.

1. Melt margarine over low heat in pot. Add evaporated milk and chocolate pieces and stir until smooth, thick and creamy. Turn off the heat and pour into a bowl and let cool slightly.
2. Skewer a banana slice, dip into warm chocolate, and then place on cookie sheet.
3. When all the fruit has been dipped, place the cookie sheet in freezer to harden the chocolate. This treat should be eaten within 24 hours.

READING:
LITTLE TOOT

Written and illustrated by Hardie Gramatky
(New York: G.P.Putnam's Sons, 1939)

Little Toot, a small tugboat, spends his days "playing" in the harbor, getting in the way of the other tugboats that are working hard, pulling big ships out to sea. His father and grandfather are famous for their strength and bravery, but Little Toot doesn't seem to be able to master any skills other than blowing lots of smoke balls and sailing in figure eights. When a big ocean liner becomes stuck on the rocks during a storm, Little Toot saves the day, forming a distress signal with his balls of smoke, alerting the entire fleet of tugboats. Although the storm prevents the other boats from reaching the ocean liner, Little Toot is able to pull the big ship to safety by riding on the top of the huge waves.

POSITIVE PARENTAL PARTICIPATION NOTE:

Growing up is a formidable task and mastering skills is a large part of that. Little Toot had to learn to channel his energy constructively. Young children need to master many skills such as dressing themselves and using the toilet, and, just like Little Toot, they also need to channel their energy in positive ways. Parents can help their children by offering loving encouragement and by acknowledging sincere efforts, even if the progress seems slow.

NOTES:

_____
_____
_____
_____
_____
_____

CRAFTING:
BIG BOAT-LITTLE BOAT COLLAGE

You will need: Pre-cut construction paper boats in various colors and sizes, paste, and a large piece of construction paper or cardboard.

1. Let your child choose a selection of paper boats of various colors and sizes.
2. Paste each boat on the large piece of paper or cardboard.
3. Talk about the different sizes and colors your child has used.

COOKING:
CHILD-FRIENDLY SMOKE-BALL
MASHED POTATOES

You will need: 2 medium-size potatoes, 1 Tb butter (or margarine), 3 Tb milk, salt and pepper to taste, potato masher, wire whisk, bowl, pot of boiling water, and an ice-cream scoop.

1. Wash the potatoes and then peel and cut into quarters.
2. Boil for 20 to 30 minutes, until tender. Drain and mash.
3. Add butter, salt and pepper and milk (you can add more milk if you like your mashed potatoes more creamy) and beat with a whisk or wooden spoon until light and fluffy.
4. Use an ice-cream scoop to dole out the "smoke-ball" portions. This recipe makes enough for two…you can easily increase the ingredients for more servings.

READING:
ALL BY MYSELF

Written and illustrated by Anna Grossnickle Hines
(New York: Clarion Books, 1985)

Josie doesn't want to wear diapers to bed anymore, but her mother explains that she will have a wet bed if she isn't able to get up to go to the bathroom. Josie is able to get up the first night, but she wets her bed the second night. Her mother is very understanding and offers to let her wear diapers for the night, but Josie decides to keep trying. Her determination pays off and two nights later, Josie is able to wake up and go to the bathroom all by herself.

POSITIVE PARENTAL PARTICIPATION NOTE:

Each child has his or her own time-line for mastering skills and tasks. Just because one child can drink from a cup at one year and is dry at night at age two does not mean that a sibling will achieve these important milestones of growing up at a similar age. In nursery school, one three-year old may be able to write his entire name quite legibly, while his four-year old classmate may have trouble with forming the letters of his first name. Patient understanding and praise for progress towards each goal will help a young child feel that his goals are attainable. Looking through a picture album showing different stages of your child's life will help him visualize how much he has already accomplished. Relating similar frustrations that you may have experienced will help your child realize that he is not alone in overcoming these same obstacles.

NOTES:

_____

_____

_____

_____

_____

_____

CRAFTING:
AN ALBUM OF ME!

You will need: A small blank photo album, a selection of photographs of your child at different stages of his life, self-stick labels, and a fine point marker.

1. With your child, go through some of the pictures that you have of him from birth to the present and let him choose several to include in his own album. Make copies of these if you want to keep the originals in the family album.
2. Help your child insert each photo and write a description (with his input) on a label, affixing it to the bottom of each page.
3. Listen while he turns the pages of his album and tells you the story of his life.

COOKING:
CHILD-FRIENDLY TURKEY BREAST AND
CHEESE SANDWICH

Young children gain a tremendous degree of self-confidence when they are able to do certain things for themselves. Knowing how to make a simple sandwich is a task worth mastering…your child will be able to fix his own lunch if you are not able to!

You will need the following for each sandwich: two slices of whole wheat (or other) bread, one or two slices of turkey breast, one slice of cheese (your choice). Optional: lettuce, tomato, sprouts, mayonnaise or mustard.

1. For each sandwich, spread mayonnaise or mustard on the bread and layer turkey slices and cheese. Add lettuce, tomato and/or sprouts if desired.
2. Cover with the other slice of bread and cut in half or quarters. Creative idea: use cookie cutters for interesting shapes!

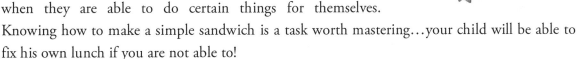

READING:
MIKE MULLIGAN AND HIS STEAM SHOVEL

Written and illustrated by Virginia Lee Burton
(Boston, Houghton Mifflin Company, 1939)

Mike Mulligan and his steam shovel named Mary Anne were a hard-working team that had helped dig the canals for ocean liners and level the fields to make landing strips for airplanes. However, technology forced them out of business as gasoline, electric and Diesel motor shovels were invented. Mike read an ad from the town of Popperville and went there with Mary Anne to apply for the job of digging the cellar for a new town hall. Although the town councilman was skeptical, he gave Mike and Mary Anne a chance with the following condition: if Mike could not complete the job in one day, the town would not have to pay him. When the whole town came to watch Mike and Mary Anne working, the steam shovel dug faster and harder than ever before and the cellar was completed by the end of the day.

POSITIVE PARENTAL PARTICIPATION NOTE:

Parents can encourage their children to help with simple household chores when they are young enough to be enthusiastic about helping. Although the job they do may not be perfect, the skills they are mastering are ones they will need throughout their lives. Most importantly, you will be fostering a sense of responsibility in your child.

NOTES:
_____
_____
_____
_____
_____
_____

CRAFTING:
WORK VEHICLE COLLAGE

You will need: Old magazines, construction paper, paste, and scissors.

1. Go through several old magazines and cut out pictures of various work vehicles (or draw some and cut them out) and paste onto construction paper.
2. Go for a walk with your child and count how many work vehicles you see.

COOKING:
CHILD-FRIENDLY MINI APPLE PIES

Young children love eating things that are sized just for them…here is a simple apple pie that your child will enjoy making for the whole family.

You will need: 1 cup chopped apples, 1 Tb sugar, ¼ tsp cinnamon, ¼ cup raisins, 1 pre-made thawed 8-inch pie crust, 1 Tb milk, a lightly greased cookie sheet, and a bowl.

1. Put the apples, sugar, raisins and cinnamon in a bowl and mix together.
2. Cut the piecrust dough in half and spoon the fruit mixture onto half of each piece.
3. Dab milk along the edges of each piece and fold the dough over the fruit.
4. Using a fork, press the edges of the crust together and prick the top several times.
5. Place each "pie" on the cookie sheet and bake at 375 degrees for 20 minutes.

Optional: In the last two or three minutes of baking, brush the tops with milk and sprinkle with sugar.

READING:
THE CARROT SEED

Written by Ruth Krauss
Illustrated by Crockett Johnson
(New York: Harper Collins Publishers, 1945)

A little boy plants a carrot seed and always remembers to water it and pull up the weeds. Although his mother, father and brother do not believe anything will grow, he continues to care for the small plot of ground where the seed was planted. His hard work and faith are rewarded when his carrot seed grows…into an enormous carrot plant and, when he pulls up the carrot, it is so big he has to use a wheelbarrow to carry it.

POSITIVE PARENTAL PARTICIPATION NOTE:

As our children face the challenges of growing up, we can encourage them (unlike the parents in this story) to face each task with enthusiasm and to work towards mastering each skill. Whether they are learning how to care for a plant or tie the laces on a pair of sneakers, our children will benefit when we maintain a positive, nurturing attitude and refrain from harsh criticism and negative comments.

NOTES:

_____

_____

_____

_____

_____

_____

_____

_____

_____

CRAFTING:
PLANT A CARROT SEED (AND A CARROT)

Taking care of a plant builds responsibility. In addition, surveys have shown that those who care for plants or pets tend to have a more positive outlook on life, lower blood pressure and better health.

You will need: 2 clean empty containers (margarine tub, milk container, etc.), potting soil, several carrot seeds, and one fresh carrot.

1. Punch several holes in the bottom of each container and fill halfway with soil.
2. Scatter several seeds on the soil in one container and press gently into the soil.
3. Cut about 1 inch of the butt (thick) end of the carrot and press, cut side down, into the soil in the other container, until covered. You can use the rest of the carrot for the carrot soup.
4. Label each container, water gently, and place in sunny windowsill. Keep moist every day and observe.

COOKING:
CHILD-FRIENDLY CARROT SOUP

Hot soup is comforting and nutritious and, when it is homemade, that is the best!

You will need: 1 Tb margarine, 1 lb carrots (peeled and sliced), 1 potato (peeled and sliced), 1 onion (diced), ½ tsp honey, 3 cups vegetable broth, dash cinnamon, 1 cup milk, fresh parsley, a large pot with a lid, and a blender.

1. Melt the margarine in pot; add veggies, cinnamon and honey.
2. Cover and cook 15 minutes on low.
3. Add the broth and simmer for 15 minutes more.
4. Puree in a blender and return to the pot, adding 1 cup of milk.
5. Heat and ladle into serving bowls. Garnish with parsley.
6. Makes 5 cups. Store leftovers in the refrigerator in a covered container.

READING:
WHISTLE FOR WILLIE

Written and illustrated by Ezra Jack Keats
(New York: Puffin Books, 1981)

A little boy named Peter wants to learn to whistle. He tries and tries to no avail. He sees another boy who whistles for his dog and the dog comes right to that boy. How Peter wishes he could do that! He hides under a box when his own dog passes by, but, because he can't whistle, his dog continues on his way. Peter practices in front of the mirror and then goes out to play again. When he sees his dog, Peter hides under the box again and tries to whistle. This time he is successful and his dog hears him. Peter is so happy and he runs home to demonstrate his new accomplishment to his proud parents.

POSITIVE PARENTAL PARTICIPATION NOTE:

How many skills do we master in our first five years of life? It is a phenomenal number! From rolling over in the crib to sitting up unaided, from taking one's first steps to walking up and down the stairs, from holding a bottle to drinking from a cup…the list goes on and on. And, each time your child masters a new skill or successfully completes a particular task, his self-esteem grows and he moves eagerly towards new challenges.

NOTES:

_____
_____
_____
_____
_____
_____
_____
_____
_____

CRAFTING:
MAKE A WHISTLING INSTRUMENT

You will need: A glass or bottle, some water and a drinking straw.

1. Hold the straw up and blow across the mouth of the straw. You will hear a whistle-like sound.
2. Fill the glass or bottle with water and lower the straw into the water. Blow across the mouth of the straw...as you move the straw up and down, the tone changes.

COOKING:
CHILD-FRIENDLY "WHISTLE WHILE YOU WORK" TORTILLA PIZZA

Pizza is a great favorite with children and adults alike. There are an infinite number of variations you can try by substituting different toppings.

You will need: (for each pizza) 1 8-inch whole wheat flour tortilla, ¼ cup pasta sauce (or ¼ cup diced canned tomatoes, drained or ¼ cup diced fresh tomato), ¼ cup shredded mozzarella cheese, 1 tsp grated Parmesan cheese, ¼ cup cooked broccoli florets (or ¼ cup diced green pepper and onion), 1 tsp olive oil, and a baking sheet.

1. Place tortilla on baking sheet. Brush with olive oil.
2. Spread pasta sauce (or tomatoes) on tortilla. Add broccoli or other veggies.
3. Top with Parmesan cheese and shredded mozzarella.

Bake at 350 degrees for about 5-7 minutes until the cheese is melted.

READING:
LEO THE LATE BLOOMER

Written by Robert Kraus
Illustrated by Jose Aruego
(New York: Windmill Books, 1971)

A little lion named Leo is unable to do the things his animal friends can do such as write his name, draw a picture, eat neatly and talk. His father is very worried and questions Leo's mother. She reassures him that Leo will learn to do everything in his own time. In the end, she is proved right and Leo masters all those skills with great finesse.

POSITIVE PARENTAL PARTICIPATION NOTE:

Parents are often tempted to compare one child in the family to another, or they read a book on child development and carefully note at what age their child should be walking or talking or mastering one skill or another. Of course, it is important to be aware of the various stages of a child's physical, intellectual and emotional development because the earlier a problem is detected, the faster help can be obtained. However, it is also important to realize that each child matures at his or her own pace.

NOTES:

_____

_____

_____

_____

_____

_____

_____

_____

_____

_____

CRAFTING:
DAISY CHAIN NECKLACE

Young children love making things for themselves and for others. Why don't you let your child make two necklaces, one for himself and one for a friend or relative.

You will need: Piece of yarn or ribbon long enough to make a necklace, transparent tape, construction paper, hole-puncher, and large macaroni or other pasta.

1. Wrap tape around one end of the yarn or ribbon and tie a piece of macaroni at the other end…this will keep the paper flowers and pasta from falling off.
2. Cut small flower shapes from construction paper and punch a hole in each.
3. Let your child string the macaroni and paper flowers, alternating each until his necklace is almost full.
4. Untie the macaroni and tie the two ends of the yarn together.

COOKING:
CHILD-FRIENDLY LION'S CANDY

These healthful candies are out-of-this-world…and so easy to make. Your child's self-esteem will bloom right before your eyes as he helps to prepare this delicious treat.

You will need: ½ cup peanut (or other nut) butter, ½ cup ground sunflower seeds, ¼ cup instant dry milk, 1 Tb honey, ½ cup of finely chopped raisins, dates or other dried fruit, ½ tsp cocoa (optional), and a large bowl.

1. Blend together nut butter and ground sunflower seeds.
2. Stir in dry milk, honey and dried fruit. Mix well (with hands, if necessary).
3. If the mixture is too dry, add some liquid milk; if too wet, add more dry milk.
4. Form into teaspoon-sized balls. Press into cocoa powder, if desired.
5. Makes about two-dozen balls. Store in an airtight container in the refrigerator.

READING:
THE LITTLE ENGINE THAT COULD

Retold by Watty Piper
Illustrated by George and Doris Hauman
(New York: Platt & Munk Publishers, 1930)

A little train is chugging along the track, bringing toys of all kinds and good things to eat to the children in the city on the other side of the mountain. When the engine breaks down, the passengers (dolls, toy soldiers, and clowns) get out and flag down various engines that pass by, asking each for help to pull their train up and over the mountain. Each engine refuses to help until finally, a little blue engine that has never gone over the mountain before agrees. As the engine moves along, she chugs, "I think I can, I think I can." The little blue engine completes her task and brings the train filled with toys and food over the mountain to the children of the city.

POSITIVE PARENTAL PARTICIPATION NOTE:

This book illustrates how important a positive attitude can be when one has a challenge to meet or a difficult obstacle to overcome. Each time our children complete a task successfully or learn a new skill, their self-esteem grows. We can help them by approaching life with a positive attitude and encouraging them to do the same.

NOTES:

_____

_____

_____

_____

_____

CRAFTING:
CONTAINER TRAIN WITH MOVING WHEELS

Most children love vehicles that move; if you both have the time and the patience, you can construct different cars to make an entire moving train…engine, coal cars, and caboose.

You will need: For each train car: 1 clean quart-sized cardboard juice or milk container, construction paper, paste, scissors, markers, and metal paper fasteners.

1. Depending on which car you want to make, cut the container appropriately (for example, for a coal car, lay the container on its side and cut off the top side).
2. Cut a piece of construction paper to fit over the outside of the container and paste.
3. Cut out four wheels from another piece of construction paper and attach to the container with paper fasteners.

Ask your child to name his train (for example, Jeremy's Express) and write the name on the side of the train car. Use markers to add details to the train.

COOKING:
CHILD-FRIENDLY HOMEMADE CHUNKY APPLESAUCE

You will need: 3 lbs tart cooking apples (peeled, cored and quartered), 1 Tb honey, ¾ cup water, 1 pinch cinnamon or nutmeg (optional), and a large saucepan with a lid.

1. Combine the apples, water and honey in the pan, cover and bring to a boil. Lower the heat and simmer, stirring frequently, until very soft and mushy (about 30 minutes).
2. Sprinkle with a little cinnamon or nutmeg if desired and serve hot or cold.

Store in a covered container in the refrigerator. Makes about 4-6 servings.

READING:
HENRY THE EXPLORER

Written by Mark Taylor
Illustrated by Graham Booth
(New York: Atheneum, 1966)

After reading a book about exploring, a little boy named Henry decides to go exploring with his dog, Angus. Henry makes a list of everything he will need, including food for himself and Angus, in case they get hungry, and a large number of paper flags so that he can mark and "claim" all of the places and things he discovers. Henry and Angus spend the entire day walking and, by the end of the day, they are far from home, near the edge of a large forest. When they decide to explore a cave, they discover a bear family and Henry realizes that it is time to go home. Darkness falls before Henry gets home and his family alerts the townspeople who start to search for Henry. However, Henry has done an excellent job of marking his trail and returns home safely by himself.

POSITIVE PARENTAL PARTICIPATION NOTE:

Childhood is the training ground for the independence that we will have as adults. Although we do not want to encourage our young children to go off by themselves as Henry did, parents might invite their child's participation in planning a family vacation or a simple outing together to discover new sites in an already familiar area. Your child might suggest (and help make) the picnic lunch, as well as list important items to take along.

NOTES:

_____
_____
_____
_____
_____

CRAFTING:
MAKE AN AMERICAN FLAG

You will need: Construction paper (red, white and blue), 1 package of gold stars, scissors, and paste.

1. Cut seven long strips, each about ½ inch wide, from the red construction paper. Paste these onto the white paper, leaving about a ½ inch space between each (this will be your 13 red and white stripes).
2. Cut a rectangle from the blue paper about 3 inches by 4 inches and paste in the upper left hand corner of the page. Fill the blue space with 50 stars.

COOKING:
CHILD-FRIENDLY PICNIC LUNCH
(PEANUT BUTTER AND JELLY SANDWICHES,
FRUIT SLICES, AND JUICE)

You will need per person: 2 slices of whole wheat bread, 1 Tb peanut butter (or any nut butter of your choice), 1 Tb jelly (or jam of your choice), ½ apple sliced, ½ orange in sections, and 1 juice box.

1. Spread the nut butter on one slice of bread and jelly on the other. Make a sandwich and cut in quarters or use cookie cutters for interesting shapes. Wrap in plastic wrap.
2. Put the apple slices and orange sections in plastic bag or small plastic container.
3. Let your child decorate a paper lunch sack and fill with sandwich, juice box, and fruit.
4. Enjoy a picnic with your child…outdoors in a park or indoors on a beach towel in your living room!

READING:
KATY AND THE BIG SNOW

Written and illustrated by Virginia Lee Burton
(Boston: Houghton Mifflin Company, 1943)

No matter what the season, Katy, the crawler tractor, helped the highway department in the city of Geoppolis. In the spring, summer and fall, she worked on fixing the roads, but in the winter, they changed the bulldozer for a snowplow. Most of the time there was not much snow so Katy spent most of her time during the winter in the garage. One day, a huge snowstorm caused all of the roads to be blocked and when the other snowplows broke down, Katy was sent out. Katy plowed the entire city and enabled the police, fire department and other emergency services to continue helping people.

POSITIVE PARENTAL PARTICIPATION NOTE:

*When it comes to mastering tasks, Katy certainly takes first prize.
By the end of the story, you and your child will be cheering for the hardworking tractor! We all need a cheering committee and you are your child's most important fan. As your child takes on new challenges and learns new skills, celebrate his successes with him and encourage him when he falls short of his goal.*

NOTES:

_____

_____

_____

_____

_____

_____

_____

_____

CRAFTING:
MAKE A COTTONBALL SNOW-CLEARED ROADWAY

You will need: A piece of cardboard or heavyweight construction paper, cotton balls, paste, and crayons or markers.

1. Help your child draw a winding road on the cardboard or construction paper.
2. Paste cotton balls all over the paper, except on the road.
3. Your child can now use a small matchbox car or truck to travel along the snow-cleared roadway.

COOKING:
CHILD-FRIENDLY HOT COCOA

Whenever I have a cup of hot cocoa, I am reminded of the day that five year-old Peter was sent home from school to change his clothes because he had gotten all wet, playing in the snow during kindergarten recess, after being warned by the teacher to stay out of the snow. I'm sure his well-meaning teacher expected me to scold him, but he returned to school with dry clothes and the experience of sharing a mug of hot cocoa, a favorite picture book, and a plate of cookies with his mother. He has grown into a wonderful, loving and responsible young man, and I know that he still remembers that day fondly. The simplest things sometimes make the greatest impression on our young children.

You will need for each cup: 1 Tb cocoa, 1 Tb sugar, ¼ cup water, ¾ cup milk, whipped cream if desired, and a small saucepan.

1. Mix cocoa and sugar in the pan and slowly stir in the water.
2. Heat over low temperature, stirring frequently, until boiling.
3. Boil slowly, stirring constantly for two minutes.
4. Add milk and heat thoroughly, but do not boil.

Pour into a mug and add a dollop of whipped cream, if desired.

READING:
GOING TO THE POTTY

Written by Fred Rogers
Photos by Jim Judkis
(New York: G.P.Putnam's Sons, 1966)

This photographic journey highlights the task for children of using the toilet. We see babies and very young toddlers being changed, fed and dressed by their parents. The author, Fred Rogers (of the famous Mister Rogers' Neighborhood television series), emphasizes that we learn to do things for ourselves as we grow up. He encourages parents to foster trust by being loving and non-judgmental in all situations.

Positive Parental Participation Note:

*As we help our children face new situations with compassion and love,
we are teaching them that they can successfully meet other challenges in the future.*

Notes:

_____

_____

_____

_____

_____

_____

_____

_____

CRAFTING:
MAKE A CLAY ROPE PENCIL HOLDER

Young children have so many skills to master…in addition to going to the bathroom in the toilet and dressing themselves, they are also learning to write. Encourage your child by providing him with pencils and other writing and drawing implements. Here is a great pencil holder your child can make to hold these important tools.

You will need: A clean, empty soup can, clay and cover-ups for the work surface.

1. Work the clay until it is smooth and pliable. Using a small piece of clay, roll it long and thin. Wind this clay rope around the can, starting at the bottom edge.
2. Continue adding pieces of clay rope until the entire can is covered.
3. Let dry and then your child can color or decorate it with markers if he wishes.

COOKING:
BUTTERMILK RICE PUDDING

Desserts and snacks can be healthful as well as delicious…providing your child with an important part of his daily nutritional needs. Instead of opting for a box of store-bought pudding mix that is loaded with sugar and preservatives, why not choose this treat.

You will need: 2 cups cooked rice, 2 cups buttermilk, 1 tsp honey, ¼ cup raisins, ½ tsp cinnamon, ¼ cup chopped nuts (optional), large bowl, and a one-quart baking dish lightly sprayed with canola oil.

1. Mix all ingredients in large bowl.
2. Pour into 1 quart baking dish.
3. Bake in 350 degree oven for 30 minutes or until lightly browned.
4. Serve warm or cold. Refrigerate leftovers in a covered container. Makes 4-6 servings.

READING:
ANGELINA BALLERINA

Written by Katherine Holabird
Illustrated by Helen Craig
(Middleton, WI: Pleasant Company Publications, 2000)

Angelina is a little mouse who only wants to dance; she never cleans up her room, she doesn't get ready for school on time, in fact, she wants to do nothing but dance. Her parents decide to allow her to take ballet lessons. Since she has the opportunity to dance during her lessons, she no longer feels the need to dance when she should be cleaning her room or getting ready for school. After many years of practice, Angelina becomes a world-famous ballet dancer.

POSITIVE PARENTAL PARTICIPATION NOTE:

Angelina's parents used a very creative strategy to help their daughter. Instead of forbidding Angelina from dancing, they encouraged her and provided her with lessons. This validated her hopes and dreams and helped Angelina to achieve her goal of becoming a professional ballerina. Olympic gold medal winners often credit a large part of their success to the parents who encouraged and supported them as they worked to attain their goals.

NOTES:
_____
_____
_____
_____
_____
_____
_____
_____
_____

CRAFTING:
CAREER COLLAGE

You will need: Old magazines, construction paper, scissors, and paste.

1. Look through some old magazines with your child and help him cut out pictures of people.
2. Talk about what kinds of jobs they might have: firefighter, teacher, dancer, etc.
3. Let your child paste the pictures on the construction paper; you can write the names of the occupations next to the pictures.

COOKING:
CHILD-FRIENDLY CHEDDAR CHEESE PUFF PIE

Mice love cheese…and so do children! This recipe is perfect for dinner; just add a crisp tossed salad and fresh fruit for dessert.

You will need: 8 slices whole wheat bread, 3 cups coarsely grated Cheddar cheese, 3 eggs (lightly beaten), 2 cups milk, a pinch of paprika, 1½ quart casserole dish sprayed with canola oil, and a large bowl.

1. Alternate layers of bread and cheese in the casserole dish, beginning with bread and ending with cheese.
2. Mix the remaining ingredients in the bowl (except paprika) and pour into the casserole dish.
3. Sprinkle with paprika and bake at 350 degrees for 40-50 minutes until puffed and golden.
4. Serve immediately. Makes four generous servings.

READING:
GOOD JOB LITTLE BEAR

Written by Martin Waddell
Illustrated by Barbara Firth
(Cambridge, MA: Candlewick Press, 1999)

Little Bear spends a day playing in the woods, climbing on rocks, bouncing on tree limbs and crossing a stream. When he falls off the tree branch and slips in the stream, Big Bear is there to rescue him, encouraging Little Bear as he learns the skills he will need to survive when he is older and on his own.

POSITIVE PARENTAL PARTICIPATION NOTE:

As your child plays, he is learning many of the skills that he will need later in life. Just like Little Bear, he needs your help and encouragement to continue, even when he experiences failure. Your unconditional love and support is the most important gift that you can give to your child.

NOTES:

_____

_____

_____

_____

_____

_____

_____

_____

_____

CRAFTING:
BOXED BEAR BOOKEND

Setting aside a shelf in your child's room for books is a wonderful way to encourage your young child's interest in reading. Here is a bookend he can make to help keep the books neat. *You will need: A brick or several rocks, a box slightly larger than the brick (like a small shoebox), brown, white and black construction paper, cardboard, clear packing tape or paste, scissors, and a black marker.*

1. Put the brick (or rocks) in the box and tape it closed. Then cover the box with brown construction paper, pasting or taping in place.
2. Cut the bear's head, hands and feet from brown construction paper, reinforcing the head with cardboard. Tape or paste onto the box in the appropriate places.
3. Cut his features (eyes, nose and mouth) from white and black construction paper and tape or paste onto the appropriate places. Use a black marker to add lines on his hands and feet for paws.

COOKING:
CHILD-FRIENDLY TEDDY BEAR PANCAKES

A favorite for breakfast, these nutritious pancakes can also double as a light supper; just add a fruit salad for dessert. *You will need: 3 Tb old fashioned quick oats, 1/3 cup water, ¼ cup flour, 1 tsp baking powder, 1 egg, slightly beaten, ½ cup milk, ¼ tsp cinnamon, 1 tsp melted margarine, ¼ cup raisins, vegetable spray, medium bowl (for microwave), small and large bowl, and a skillet.*

1. Mix oats and water in the medium bowl. Microwave on high for 1 minute.
2. Combine the flour and baking powder in the small bowl.
3. Combine the egg, milk, margarine and oatmeal in the large bowl.
4. Gradually add the flour mixture to the liquid mixture, stirring to moisten.
5. Spray a skillet with vegetable spray and then heat on medium.
6. When the pan is hot, spoon 2 Tb of batter for the head and 1 tsp for each ear.
7. When top of each pancake is bubbling, turn and continue to cook until the underside is brown. Add raisins for the eyes, nose and a smiling mouth. Makes 5 or 6 pancakes.

READING:
THE COUNTRY BUNNY AND THE LITTLE GOLD SHOES

Written by DuBose Heyward
Illustrated by Marjorie Flack
(Boston: Houghton Mifflin Company, 1939)

A young country bunny sets a goal for herself of becoming one of the five Easter bunnies who deliver Easter eggs all over the world. It seems that her dreams will not be realized as the little bunny grows up and becomes a mother of twenty-one baby bunnies who keep her very busy. However, she trains each bunny to master certain skills such as cleaning the house, mending the clothes and cooking the food. When it is time for a new Easter bunny to be chosen, Little Cottontail Mother proves that she is the kindest, wisest and fastest bunny in the whole world. She is picked to fill the position and on Easter eve, she joins the other four Easter bunnies and is able to deliver all the eggs, completing the tasks assigned to her. She is rewarded with a pair of golden shoes that enable her to fly.

POSITIVE PARENTAL PARTICIPATION NOTE:

How many of us feel we are doing our children a favor by picking up after them and not requiring them to help with chores? This is no favor at all! Even the youngest toddler is old enough to learn responsibility. Making a game of picking up toys helps the job go faster; perhaps you can sing a song with your child (as Mother Cottontail had some of her children sing and dance to entertain the others while they worked) or put on some lovely classical music and dance with your child as you both dust the living room furniture.
Even Snow White's seven dwarves whistled while they worked!

NOTES:

_____

_____

_____

_____

CRAFTING:
SHOE COLLAGE

You will need: Old magazines, construction paper, paste, and scissors.

1. Help your child cut out pictures of shoes from several magazines.
2. Let him paste them on a sheet of construction paper...have him tell you the style (sneakers, pointy, sandals) or the colors and write the words next to each picture.

COOKING:
CHILD-FRIENDLY "PIE-LESS" VEGETABLE POT PIE

You will need: 4 cups mixed cooked vegetables (potatoes, carrots, green beans, whatever your family likes or you have left over), 14 oz of creamy potato leek soup (I use Imagine brand), ½ cup water, and a 6-cup casserole dish.

1. Mix the veggies (if the vegetables are raw, boil them in a minimum amount of water for 5 minutes and drain; if they are frozen, you can just add them to bowl), soup and water in a bowl and spoon into the casserole dish.
2. Bake at 350 degrees for 35-40 minutes until bubbling.

Serves 4-6.

READING:
DRY DAYS, WET NIGHTS

Written by Marbeth Boelts
Illustrated by Kathy Parkinson
(Morton Grove, IL: Albert Whitman & Company, 1994)

Little Bunny is gradually mastering many skills and tasks. He can wash himself in the tub, brush his own teeth and use the bathroom by himself. Staying dry at night, however, is a big challenge and, although Little Bunny is sad that he cannot get up in time to use the bathroom, his parents are understanding about his wetting the bed and encourage him not to give up hope. They explain that many other bunnies wet their beds at night and Little Bunny's father even confides that when he was young, he also had trouble waking up in order to use the bathroom. At the end of the story, Little Bunny attains his goal of staying dry all night.

POSITIVE PARENTAL PARTICIPATION NOTE:

We never stop learning and our bodies are changing all the time. Parents need to reassure their children when they fall short of a goal. Each child matures at his or her own individual pace and using anger and humiliation are not productive ways to encourage a child to master a skill or task.

NOTES:

_____

_____

_____

_____

_____

_____

_____

CRAFTING:
MAKE A STAR-STUDDED GOAL CHART

You will need: A piece of construction paper, a package of stars, markers or crayons, old magazines, scissors and paste.

1. Talk to your child about some of the skills and tasks that he is trying to master.
2. Divide the paper into sections and label each section with a different skill or task. If possible, paste a picture from a magazine or draw a picture that shows that particular skill or task.
3. Each time your child makes progress towards his goal, place a star sticker in that section.

COOKING:
CHILD-FRIENDLY PEANUT BUTTER BALLS

When my children were small, this was one of their favorite treats…both to make and to eat!

You will need: ¼ cup peanut butter, ¼ cup honey, ½ cup non-fat dried milk powder, ¼ cup shredded coconut, a large bowl, and a cookie sheet lined with wax paper.

1. Mix the first three ingredients in a large bowl until well blended. Then roll into small balls (about one tablespoonful each).
2. Roll the balls in shredded coconut and place on waxed paper.
3. Refrigerate for 15 to 20 minutes.
4. Place uneaten balls in a covered Tupperware-type container and store in the refrigerator for up to a week (although they won't remain uneaten for that long).
5. This recipe makes about one dozen balls. You can double or quadruple the recipe quite easily.

READING:
CORNELIUS P. MUD, ARE YOU READY FOR BED?

Written and illustrated by Barney Saltzberg
(Cambridge, MA: Candlewick Press, 2005)

It's time for bed and Cornelius' father asks him the questions which we all ask our children at bedtime…have you put away your toys, have you used the bathroom, have you brushed your teeth, have you put on your pajamas? Although the little pig answers each question with a "yes", the charming illustrations show that he and his father have different ideas about what needs to be done in order to get ready for bed. Cornelius' understanding father accepts his son's somewhat strange routine and makes sure that he doesn't forget the most important thing…a loving hug from him.

POSITIVE PARENTAL PARTICIPATION NOTE:

Young children very much want to become independent and, although they may put their pajamas on backwards, we need to encourage them to learn to do things by themselves. Of course, parents need to supervise some tasks; we don't want them swallowing the whole tube of toothpaste or emptying the entire box of fish food into the aquarium. However, praise for good effort encourages a child to keep trying and, as your child masters each task and skill, his self-esteem grows.

NOTES:

_____
_____
_____
_____
_____
_____
_____

CRAFTING:
A NO TICK-TOCK CLOCK

Bedtime is a very special time for young children, but without routines and limits, many try to delay going to bed as much as possible. With your help, your child can "set" his clock to the particular time when he will need to be ready for his bedtime story. Then he can check that time against the real clocks in the house and will know when he has to complete his toy cleanup in order to be ready for that special treat…the bedtime story.

You will need: A piece of cardboard (from a cereal box), metal paper fastener, construction paper, marker, and scissors.

1. Cut a large circle (the clock face) from the cardboard.
2. Cut two "hands" (one longer and narrower than the other) from the construction paper.
3. Attach the hands to the center of the clock with the paper fastener.
4. Draw the numbers in the correct order on the clock face.

COOKING:
CHILD-FRIENDLY OVERNIGHT COOKIES

This recipe is unique as the cookies remain in the oven overnight and are ready in the morning…perhaps your child can have one with breakfast as a special treat…the egg whites, raisins and chopped nuts provide high quality nutrition.

You will need: 2 egg whites, ¼ cup sugar, 1 cup finely chopped nuts, 1 cup of raisins, aluminum foil, cookie sheet, canola oil spray, electric mixer, and a large bowl.

1. Beat the egg whites with the electric mixer until stiff. Add the sugar slowly.
2. Fold in the nuts and raisins. Line the cookie sheet with foil and spray with oil.
3. Drop mixture by the teaspoonful onto the sheet and press down gently.
4. Bake at 350 degrees for 5 minutes. Turn oven off.
5. Remove cookie sheet from oven in the morning and slide cookies off the sheet. Store in an airtight container.

READING:
I CAN DO IT TOO!

Written by Karen Baicker
Illustrated by Ken Wilson-Max
(New York: Handprint Books, 2003)

Vibrant pictures help tell the story of a little girl who is learning to master many tasks and skills. Although her sweater may not be perfectly buttoned and she spills a little juice while pouring it into her own glass, she is very proud that she can do these things by herself. Her family stands ready to offer support, encouragement and praise, and the little girl is able to offer the same encouragement to her younger brother.

POSITIVE PARENTAL PARTICIPATION NOTE:

As parents, we help our young children master tasks and skills. We need to remember to praise them lavishly and to refrain from harsh criticism. Young children need a great deal of support and encouragement to try to do new things.

NOTES:

_____

_____

_____

_____

_____

_____

_____

_____

_____

CRAFTING:
CAN DO COLLAGE

You will need: Old magazines, piece of construction paper, paste, and scissors.

1. Talk to your child about the various tasks and skills he has mastered already (picking up his toys, brushing his teeth, helping to set the dinner table, buttoning his clothes, etc.) and look through the magazines for pictures that help to illustrate those accomplishments.
2. Cut the pictures out of the magazines and paste onto the paper.
3. At the top of the paper or in the center, write a title for the collage (i.e. This Is What I Can Do!).
4. Hang the collage in a place of honor in your home…what a boost to your child's self-esteem!

COOKING:
CHILD-FRIENDLY FRESHLY-SQUEEZED ORANGE JUICE

Young children need to learn that the foods that we eat and drink all have original sources…frozen, canned or packaged orange juice pales in comparison to this treat!

You will need: For each 6 oz glass of juice: 1 or 2 oranges (depending on the size) and a manual juicer if available.

1. Wash the oranges under cold water.
2. Cut each orange in half.
3. If you have a manual juicer, press each orange half onto it and rotate to release all of the juice. If you don't have a manual juicer, you can squeeze as much juice as possible out of each half…it will be a bit messier this way.
4. Carefully spoon out any pits.
5. Pour into a glass and enjoy!

NOTES:

CHAPTER TWO: "I'M SPECIAL!"

How to help your child value his own strengths and qualities

The summer Head Start program was well underway when four-year old Lorraine and her family moved into the neighborhood. Seven pairs of eyes focused on the commotion in the front of the room as Lorraine's mother hugged her daughter and left. As Lorraine apprehensively watched the other children from her wheelchair, I played the story time chords on the piano and seven three and four-year olds hurried to sit down in the library corner. As I moved Lorraine into position next to the other children, three-year old William called out, "That's a funny chair. It has wheels." "Yes," I explained. "Lorraine's wheelchair helps her get around because her legs aren't strong enough for her to be able to walk. But even though her legs are not strong, her memory is. Let's take turns telling Lorraine our names and our favorite flavor ice cream and, after our story, we will have a welcome-to-our-class party for Lorraine with ice cream as a special treat. We will see if she can remember which flavor each of you likes best." I glanced at Lorraine and was happy to see that she looked delighted to be able to showcase one of her talents. After each smiling child had called out his name and favorite flavor, I opened *Crow Boy* by Taro Yashima and added, "Each of us is unique and different in very special ways. I have a wonderful story about a little boy and his classmates in a school far away."

> *"Do you know what you are? You are unique. In all the world there is no child exactly like you."*
> *Pablo Casals*

POSITIVE PARENTAL PARTICIPATION NOTE:

All too often, we are encouraged to conform to the "norm" and, in turn, we expect our children to do the same. Life becomes a paint-by-number picture and our children must color the leaves green and the sky blue in order to win our praise. We can help our children develop strong positive self-images by allowing them to express their individuality, whether it means we allow them to color the leaves purple and the sky yellow or we encourage them to pursue an interest that is different from those of the rest of the family.

READING:
INCREDIBLE ME!

Written by Kathi Appelt
Illustrated by Brian Karas
(New York: Harper Collins Publishers, 2003)

This book is a celebration of the uniqueness of each individual. The main (and only) character of the uplifting rhyme is a little girl whose smile and nose and kiss and toes are like no one else's.

POSITIVE PARENTAL PARTICIPATION NOTE:

As a parent, you have an enormous impact on how your child thinks of himself and others. When parents focus positively on their child's unique qualities that impact is a constructive one and helps build a positive self-image. The main characters in each of the stories in this chapter learn to value their special qualities and strengths and, by reading each story and participating in the accompanying art activity and cooking experience, you will be able to foster high self-esteem in your children as well.

NOTES:
_____
_____
_____
_____
_____
_____
_____
_____

CRAFTING:
ALUMINUM FOIL MIRROR-IN-A-FRAME

You will need: A sheet of aluminum foil (about 6x6 inches), a piece of cardboard (about 7x7 inches), sequins, paste, and a piece of ribbon for hanging.

1. Spread paste on one side of the cardboard. Carefully center the aluminum foil and press down.
2. Press sequins into the space around the aluminum foil for a beautiful border.
3. Instead of sequins, you could use buttons or macaroni.
4. To hang: punch a hole in each top corner and attach a ribbon.

COOKING:
CHILD-FRIENDLY STRUDEL WITH APPLES AND JAM

You will need: 4 or 5 thawed sheets of phyllo dough (frozen food section in most stores), ½ cup warmed jam (strawberry, apricot or raspberry), 2 cups apples (peeled and chopped), ¾ cup raisins, 3 Tb melted butter or margarine, ¼ cup toasted fine bread crumbs, a small amount of flour, and a baking sheet sprayed with canola oil.

1. Lay the stack of 4 or 5 phyllo sheets onto the baking sheet.
2. Brush with 2 Tb melted butter and scatter the breadcrumbs on top.
3. Spread the warmed jam over the crumbs and spoon raisins and apples down the middle, leaving 3 inches on each side.
4. Fold the sides over the filling and brush 1 Tb of melted butter on top.
5. Transfer carefully to baking sheet and brush the top with melted butter.
6. Bake at 350 degrees for 40 to 50 minutes.
7. Serves 12. Wrap unused portion in foil and store in the refrigerator.

READING:
LENTIL

Written and illustrated by Robert McCloskey
(New York: Viking Press, 1940)

In a small town, a young boy named Lentil learns to play the harmonica because he loves music, but cannot sing. The townspeople plan a wonderful celebration for the arrival of Colonel Carter, a very important contributor to the town. Unfortunately, one of Colonel Carter's former classmates tries to sabotage the grand welcome by preventing the band from performing. Lentil comes to the rescue by entertaining Colonel Carter with harmonica music.

POSITIVE PARENTAL PARTICIPATION NOTE:

One person definitely can make a difference! Lentil used his love of music and gift for playing the harmonica to help the townspeople. We must help our children learn to value their strengths and special qualities. If we praise them and encourage them, they will believe in themselves and look forward to new challenges as they grow.

NOTES:
_____
_____
_____
_____
_____
_____
_____
_____
_____
_____

CRAFTING:
MAKE A WAXED PAPER KAZOO

Children love music…listening to it, dancing to it, singing with it and making it…you can help your child make an instrument so he can create his own music. *You will need: A sheet of waxed paper and a clean comb.*

1. Fold a piece of waxed paper around the comb.
2. See what kind of music your child can make by humming into the waxed paper.
3. Different sized combs will produce different sounds.

COOKING:
CHILD-FRIENDLY PUCKER-UP LEMON BREAD

Does looking at a lemon make you pucker up? Try this experiment with your young child…take a fresh lemon, wash it off, think about what it would taste like, cut a slice or two, smell it…are you salivating yet? If not, try a taste…I'm sure it will make you pucker up, just like the members of the band in Lentil's hometown. Now you can use the rest of the lemon to make this delicious bread!

You will need: ½ cup canola oil, ½ cup honey, 2 eggs, 2¼ cups flour, 2 tsp baking powder, the zest of 1 lemon, ½ cup chopped nuts (optional), 1 cup milk, 9 inch loaf pan (lightly greased), and a large bowl. For the topping you will need: the juice of a lemon and ¼ cup sugar.

1. Mix all ingredients together (except topping ingredients) and spoon into prepared loaf pan.
2. Bake at 325 degrees for 40 minutes.
3. Mix the juice of the lemon and ¼ cup sugar until the sugar dissolves.

When you remove the bread from the oven, prick the top of the loaf with a toothpick and then pour on the lemon and sugar mixture… it will penetrate the entire loaf of bread and each slice will be brimming with lemon flavor!

READING:
BRAVO MAURICE

Written and illustrated by Rebecca Bond
(Boston: Little Brown & Company, 2000)

When Maurice is born, his family members are convinced that he will grow up to be just like each of them. His father, who is a baker, is sure that Maurice has the big hands needed to become a good baker. His grandmother believes that Maurice has a nose just like hers and that means he will be a wonderful gardener. As Maurice grows up, the members of his family make sure he has an opportunity to try doing the things they love to do. However, at a very young age, Maurice is always singing and even though each member of his family is anxious for Maurice to love to do what they love to do, they are all thrilled and excited when they realize that Maurice's special gift is for singing.

POSITIVE PARENTAL PARTICIPATION NOTE:

It is so important to provide a variety of activities for young children…always encouraging, but never pressuring or pushing them to participate. Sometimes a reluctant child will gain enough courage to take part in an activity when his parent happily participates also.

NOTES:
_____
_____
_____
_____
_____
_____
_____
_____

CRAFTING:
DECORATE A MILK CARTON PLANTER

Just like Maurice, most young children are fascinated with growing things…you can help your child decorate a milk carton that will hold a tiny herb garden.

You will need: 1 half-gallon cardboard milk or juice carton, potting soil, herb seedlings from a local garden shop (parsley, basil, oregano, etc.), a nail for making holes in the bottom of the carton, wallpaper border or wallpaper samples, and paste.

1. Cut the milk carton in half (length-wise) and poke holes in the bottom.
2. Cut the wallpaper to fit the outside of the carton and paste in place.
3. Fill the carton with soil about halfway and plant the seedlings.
4. Set the carton in a plastic tray to protect surfaces from water damage. Water carefully so the soil is moist, but not soggy.
5. Place in a sunny windowsill and water when needed.

COOKING:
CHILD-FRIENDLY HERB BREAD

When your child's herb garden is in full bloom, you will be able to use cuttings to flavor the meals you prepare. For this bread, you will have to use store-bought herbs.

You will need: 3 cups flour, 1 tsp salt, 4½ tsp baking powder, 3 Tb sugar, 1 Tb herb blend (oregano, basil, parsley, rosemary, thyme…your choice), 12 oz milk, a large bowl, and a 9x5 inch loaf pan greased.

1. In a large bowl, mix the flour, salt, baking powder, sugar and herb blend.
2. Stir in the milk.
3. Turn the batter into the loaf pan and bake for 60 minutes at 325 degrees.
4. Turn out and cool on rack…delicious toasted or not.

READING:
YES WE CAN!

Written by Sam McBratney
Illustrated by Charles Fuge
(New York: HarperCollins Publishers, 2006)

Little Roo, Country Mouse and Quacker Duck start to make a giant pile of leaves, but stop to rest. While they are resting, they start making fun of each other for what they don't do well until Roo's mother suggests they each show what they can do best. Little Roo jumps over a log, Quacker Duck floats on a puddle, and Country Mouse chases and catches his own tail. The friends agree that each one is special and has unique talents and qualities.

POSITIVE PARENTAL PARTICIPATION NOTE:

Little Roo's mother found a creative way to teach her son and his friends to appreciate their own special talents without envying those of others. As parents, we need to encourage our children to value their own strengths and qualities, as well as the strengths and qualities of others. We make a start by recognizing their uniqueness and supporting their creativity, even if it veers in a different direction from ours.

NOTES:

_____

_____

_____

_____

_____

_____

_____

_____

_____

CRAFTING:
LEAF PRINTS

This is a lovely fall project as there will be many leaves on the ground to choose from. However, one can find leaves during almost every season. During a nature walk with your child, take a plastic bag and help him pick several different kinds of leaves...remember, if they are too brittle, they will fall to pieces. *You will need: Several leaves of different sizes and shapes, small bowls of tempera paint (check your local art supply store for non-toxic varieties), construction paper, and cover-ups for work surface and workers.*

1. Use the cover-ups for work surface and workers and then briefly lay one of the leaves in the paint, put on the paper, cover with another piece of paper and press.
2. Your child can make leaf prints using one leaf and many colors, many leaves and one color, or a combination of both.
3. Observe with your child how each leaf is unique and beautiful in its own way.

COOKING:
SURPRISE BREAD PUDDING

Just as there are many different kinds of leaves, there are many different types of bread...save a slice or two in the freezer (maybe the ends) from several different loaves...raisin, whole wheat, buttermilk, potato, white. When you are ready to make this recipe, take out 3 cups worth and defrost and tear into small pieces. Each time you make it, the taste will be unique, depending on what types of bread you used. *You will need: 3 cups of bread pieces, 2 cups milk, ¼ cup canola oil, ¼ cup honey, 2 eggs (slightly beaten), 1 tsp cinnamon, ½ cup seedless raisins, 1½ quart baking dish, and a larger baking pan with 1 inch of hot water.*

1. Put the bread in the baking dish and blend in the remaining ingredients.
2. Put the baking dish in the pan with the hot water and bake at 350 degrees for about an hour or until a knife comes out clean when inserted in the middle.
3. Makes 6 to 8 servings. Serve warm or cold.

READING:
SHY CHARLES

Written and illustrated by Rosemary Wells
(New York: Penguin Books, 1988)

Charles is an extremely shy mouse. He refuses to talk to his mother's friends and prefers to play by himself. His parents decide to force their son to change, so his mother enrolls him in ballet school and his father tries to make him join the football team, but their attempts do not improve the situation. When his parents go out for the evening, the babysitter falls down the stairs and Charles is able to respond to the emergency with courage and commonsense, proving that shyness does not prevent him from being a hero. Charles' parents realize that although their son is not outgoing, he has other important strengths and qualities.

POSITIVE PARENTAL PARTICIPATION NOTE:

Many parents try to mold their young children to follow their own interests...although there is nothing wrong in exposing our children to the activities we are passionate about (sports or bird watching, for example), we need to be on guard not to push or pressure them. In addition, we need to be sensitive to the interests they evince and be quick to encourage them, even if those interests are not the same as ours.

NOTES:

_____

_____

_____

_____

_____

_____

_____

_____

_____

CRAFTING:
EMERGENCY CONTACT LIST

This all-important list should be found near each phone…in a prominent place, not hidden under a bunch of papers!

You will need: A blank piece of writing paper, a piece of construction paper, paste, old magazines, small photos of people on your contact list, a pen and scissors.

1. Cut the copy paper so that it fits on the construction paper with a one-inch border.
2. Put paste around the edges of the copy paper and press down.
3. In large clear letters and numbers, write the important contact numbers for your family. Don't confuse the issue by listing too many…911, a close family member, a next-door neighbor, and a spouse's work or cell number would probably be enough for a young child.
4. Next to each name and number, put the picture of that person (for 911 you might put the picture of a policeman or fireman).
5. Most importantly, talk to your child about emergencies and allow him to practice dialing the phone. Have mock emergency drills as a weekly activity. Your child will gain more confidence when he knows he is capable of handling different situations.

COOKING:
CHOCOLATE COVERED STRAWBERRIES

You will need: 12 fresh strawberries washed and dried (with stems if possible, otherwise you can use toothpicks to dip), 4 oz of dark chocolate (at least 70% cocoa…full of antioxidants), a double boiler, and a cookie sheet lined with wax paper.

1. Melt the chocolate over hot water in a double boiler on low, stirring occasionally.
2. Remove the pot from the stove (but keep over the hot water). Dip each strawberry holding the stem in your hand (or use a toothpick).
3. Place the dipped fruit on a wax paper covered cookie sheet and chill until the chocolate hardens. Store in an airtight container in the refrigerator.

READING:
THE LITTLE FIR TREE

Written by Margaret Wise Brown
Illustrated by Jim LaMarche
(USA: HarperCollins Publishers, 2005)

A loving father goes into the woods and carefully digs up a young fir tree. He brings it back to his invalid son who is unable to get up from bed. Then the family decorates the tree for Christmas. In the spring, the man replants the tree in the woods and this tradition is repeated the next winter. The third winter, however, the young boy is able to walk and the entire family goes into the woods and decorates the fir tree there.

POSITIVE PARENTAL PARTICIPATION NOTE:

Even though the little fir tree questions his own value and wishes he were part of the forest instead of being all by himself, he is chosen because he is just the right size to be dug up and replanted. Young children often question their own value and worry whether they are "smart" enough or "big" enough or "good" enough. Parents need to celebrate the special qualities of their children and help them accept and embrace their own strengths.

NOTES:

_____

_____

_____

_____

_____

_____

_____

_____

_____

CRAFTING:
CHRISTMAS TREE CHAINS

Of course it is easy to buy our holiday decorations at the store…but how much more fun to make them ourselves…by changing the color of the construction paper, these chains can be used to decorate the house for many different special occasions. *You will need: Construction paper in red and green (for Christmas), scissors, and paste.*

1. Cut the construction paper into strips…the look of the chains will depend on how long and wide you cut the strips.
2. Paste the ends of one of the strips together. Loop another strip through and paste those ends together. Continue in this manner until the chain is the desired length.
3. You can alternate the colors or make chains of one single color. Hang from the ceiling, around the doorframe or on the tree.

COOKING:
"FROSTED" ORANGE SESAME MINI-MUFFINS

Baking cookies or muffins (and then decorating them) was one of my children's favorite holiday activities.

You will need: 1½ cups whole wheat flour, ½ cup white flour, ¼ cup ground sesame seeds, 2 tsp baking powder, 2 eggs, ½ cup yogurt, ¼ cup canola oil, ½ cup honey, 1 Tb grated orange zest, juice of 1 orange, 2 bowls, 1 oiled mini muffin pan (or use paper inserts instead of the oil) an electric mixer, whipped cream cheese, and raisins.

1. Mix together the flours, ground sesame seeds and baking powder.
2. With an electric mixer, beat eggs, yogurt, oil, honey, orange peel and orange juice and add to dry ingredients. Gently blend well and fill muffin cups two-thirds full.
3. Bake at 375 degrees on the top rack for 15-20 minutes until muffins are golden.
4. When cool, "frost" the muffins with cream cheese and decorate with raisins.
5. Store muffins in airtight containers in the refrigerator…perhaps some can be given to older neighbors or relatives as a holiday gift. Makes two dozen.

READING:
A GIFT-BEAR FOR THE KING

Written by Carl Memling
Illustrated by Lillian Hoban
(New York: E.P. Dutton & Company, Inc., 1966)

A very talented bear-cub is sent as a birthday gift for the king by a loving old couple. As the bear cub journeys to reach the king, he meets and helps many people. However, when he finally arrives at the palace, the king's birthday has passed and the guards lock him up in the dungeon because he is so late. While in his prison cell, the bear cub sings a sad and beautiful song about his travels. Several birds overhear him and fly off, singing the same sweet song. All of the people, whom the bear-cub had helped, come to speak to the king to explain what had happened. The king releases the bear-cub and accompanies him to the cottage of the old couple where he invites them all to live in the palace.

POSITIVE PARENTAL PARTICIPATION NOTE:

The bear-cub was special enough to be given as a birthday gift for a king! He had many qualities and strengths...he could sing, stand on his front paws and wash dishes. Every child is very special also and parents must find ways to recognize the strengths and qualities of their children.

NOTES:

_____

_____

_____

_____

_____

_____

_____

_____

_____

CRAFTING:
KING OR QUEEN FOR A DAY CROWN

I'm sure most of you reading this book are too young to remember the television show, "Queen For A Day". It was a wonderful idea that celebrated the life of one particular lady, and all the women watching could imagine they were wearing the crown. We can help our children feel special as well…perhaps the person wearing the crown gets to choose the dinner menu or the story that will be read at bedtime. (Maybe Mom, Dad and other siblings can get a chance to wear the crown also.)

You will need: A piece of construction paper, crayons, paste or tape, a sheet of colorful stars, and scissors.

1. Cut several strips of construction paper and use tape or paste to attach the strips together and fit to the size of your child's head.
2. Decorate with crayons and stars. Cut along the top to make points, if desired.

COOKING:
CHILD-FRIENDLY TRAVELING TRAIL MIX

Great to have on hand…keep several zip-lock bagsful to grab when you have to run out to the store with your child…a healthier alternative to candy bars and chips!

You will need: 2 cups Corn Chex, 2 Cups Wheat Chex, 2 cups Rice Chex, 2 cups pretzels (thin sticks), 1½ cups mixed nuts or peanuts (optional), 1 Tb margarine, 2 tsp Braggs Aminos or soy sauce and a 13x9x2 inch baking dish.

1. Melt the margarine, mix with Braggs Aminos or soy sauce and pour into the baking dish.
2. Add the cereals, pretzels and nuts, mix thoroughly to coat and microwave on high for 3 minutes.
3. Stir and continue to heat in the microwave, one minute at a time, until evenly toasted.
4. Makes about 2½ quarts. Store in an airtight container.

READING:
THE LITTLE RED CABOOSE

Written by Marian Potter
Illustrated by Tibor Gergerly
(Racine, WI: Western Publishing Company, 1953)

The little red caboose is sad because he always comes at the end of the long line of cars of the train and, by the time he passes, the people who are watching and waving at the train are already turning away. One day, the train tries to climb a big steep mountain and the locomotive is unable to keep up the momentum. When all the cars of the train begin to slip back, the little red caboose is able to set his brakes and hold them in place until two strong locomotives arrive to help push the train up and over the mountain track. From then on, because of his heroic actions, the people who come to watch and wave at the train always stay to cheer for the little red caboose.

POSITIVE PARENTAL PARTICIPATION NOTE:

Everyone needs applause...young children most of all. Our children need to hear us praise their achievements and approve their ideas. They need to feel we enjoy working together with them on projects. They need to have us participate positively with them on a daily basis. This is how we help them to feel "special" and, when they feel special, their self-esteem grows.

NOTES:

_____
_____
_____
_____
_____
_____
_____

CRAFTING:
GEOMETRIC TRAIN

Most activities are multi-learning ones…your child is mastering cutting (if he is old enough) and pasting, as well as learning to follow directions and understand spatial relationships. In addition, with this project, he is also learning about shapes and colors.

You will need: Several sheets of construction paper in different colors, paste, scissors, paper fasteners (optional), and a marker or crayons.

1. Cut several small rectangles (the train cars, locomotive, caboose) and 2 small circles for each rectangle (the wheels), and several very small squares (the windows).
2. Paste the rectangles on a big piece of construction paper leaving a small space between each. Paste two wheels at the bottom of each rectangle or attach with paper fasteners for "movable" wheels. Paste on the squares for windows.
3. Use the marker or crayons to add details to the picture (railroad tracks, doors, people riding on the train, and cables to attach the cars to each other).

COOKING:
CHILD-FRIENDLY CRUMB CAKE CABOOSE

You will need: 1 cup brown sugar, 2½ cups flour, ½ cup canola oil, 1 egg, 1 cup buttermilk, 1 tsp baking soda, 1 tsp vanilla, ¼ cup applesauce, ½ tsp cinnamon, 1 banana, a large bowl, and a 9 inch loaf pan (lightly sprayed with canola oil and then floured).

1. In a large bowl, mix the brown sugar, flour, cinnamon and oil together until they look like crumbs. Reserve ¾ cup for the topping.
2. Add the egg, buttermilk, baking soda, applesauce and vanilla and beat well.
3. Put in loaf pan and spread reserved crumbs on top.
4. Bake at 350 degrees for 45-55 minutes. Cool on a wire rack.
5. To make the caboose: cut a slice and lay it flat on a plate. Arrange slices of banana for the wheels.

READING:

DO YOU STILL LOVE ME?

Written and illustrated by Charlotte Middleton
(Cambridge, MA: Candlewick Press, 2002)

Dudley, the dog, loves his life because everyone loves him. When a new animal comes to live in his house, Dudley feels that no one pays attention to him anymore and he feels sad and unloved. When Dudley saves the life of the new pet, his family realizes how important he is to them and they begin to treat him with loving attention again.

POSITIVE PARENTAL PARTICIPATION NOTE:

It is important for parents to create opportunities for their young children to shine…telling our children they are smart and wonderful and clever is only part of the formula for helping build high self-esteem…they must actually complete tasks and reach goals as well.

NOTES:

_____
_____
_____
_____
_____
_____
_____
_____
_____
_____
_____
_____

CRAFTING:
PET COLLAGE

You will need: Old magazines, construction paper, paste, and scissors.

1. Look through old magazines with your child and help him choose and cut out pictures of animals that might be kept as pets.
2. Paste the pictures on the paper.
3. Talk about different pets, how they help us and how we help them.
4. Hang up your child's picture in a place of honor.

COOKING:
CHILD-FRIENDLY CREAM OF TOMATO SOUP WITH ANIMAL CRACKERS

Homemade cream of tomato soup...delicious, nutritious and none of the preservatives and excess salt you find in most canned varieties!

You will need: 4 cups chopped tomatoes (you can substitute canned diced tomatoes...just make sure you get the "no salt" variety), 1 Tb onion flakes, 1 Tb honey, 1 cup milk, a large pot, yogurt or sour cream (optional), and store-bought animal crackers.

1. Blend tomatoes, onion flakes and honey together in a pot.
2. Heat to just boiling. Turn to low, cover and simmer 10 minutes.
3. Stir in milk and heat on low 5 more minutes.
4. Puree in blender, if desired or leave as is for a more "chunky" soup.
5. Makes 1 quart. Serve with dollop of yogurt or sour cream, if desired.
6. Float animal crackers on top of each serving. Serves 4-6.
7. Store the leftovers in an airtight container in the refrigerator.

READING:
SWIMMY

Written and illustrated by Leo Lionni
(New York: Alfred Knopf, 1963)

One day, a big hungry tuna fish swallows an entire school of little red fish. Swimmy, the only little black fish in that school, escapes because he is the fastest swimmer. Although he is very sad to have lost his family, he enjoys discovering the many wonders of the underwater world as he swims along. When he discovers another school of little red fish hiding in the shadows of some rocks, Swimmy invites them to join him on his journey, but they are afraid to venture out of their safe haven because they will become prey to the larger fish. Swimmy decides to fool the other sea creatures by teaching the little red fish to swim together in the form of a large fish with himself as the eye, and this enables them all to leave their hiding place and enjoy the wonders of the ocean.

POSITIVE PARENTAL PARTICIPATION NOTE:

Swimmy's speed enabled him to escape the hungry tuna, his color helped him to be the "eye" of the fish formation, and his ingenuity created the idea that would save his newly found school of little red fish. Our children have special qualities also, and we must encourage them to value those strengths.

NOTES:

_____

_____

_____

_____

_____

_____

_____

_____

_____

CRAFTING:
WATERCOLOR WASH PICTURE

You will need: White construction or painting paper, a few drops of "blueberry ink", small container, water, markers, old magazines, paste, scissors, brushes, and newspapers and old shirts to cover the work surface and the workers.

1. If possible, find pictures in old magazines of fish and plants and cut them out and paste on the paper. Your child can draw his own fish and plants if he can't find any to cut out.
2. Take a drop or two of blueberry ink (made by crushing a handful of blueberries in a bowl) and mix it with water in a small container...brush this watery blue over the entire picture...it will look like an underwater wonderland.

COOKING:
CHILD-FRIENDLY FISH CASSEROLE FROM THE SEVEN SEAS

You will need: 10 oz of creamy potato leek soup, 1¼ cups milk, 1¼ cups uncooked rice, 1 can tuna (drained), 1 box frozen peas, ¼ lb sliced American cheese, 2 quart casserole dish with cover (or use aluminum foil) and a sauce pan.

1. Mix the soup and milk in the pan and bring to boil.
2. Put ½ of the soup mixture into a casserole dish and add the rice, tuna and peas.
3. Pour in the remaining soup mixture and top with cheese slices.
4. Cover and bake at 375 degrees for 20-30 minutes or until the liquid is absorbed and the rice is tender.
5. Serves 4. Add a salad and fresh whole-wheat rolls for a lovely dinner.

READING:
CROW BOY

Written and illustrated by Taro Yashima
(New York: The Viking Press, 1955)

Many years ago, in a small village school in the countryside of Japan, a young boy attends class. Chibi is always perceived as stupid and is treated as an outcast by the other students. When a new teacher, Mr. Isobe, is put in charge of the class during the final sixth year of school, the other children come to appreciate the special qualities of Chibi. Mr. Isobe recognizes how much knowledge Chibi has about growing things and animals, and he praises Chibi's artistic talent as well. The teacher takes the time to talk to the little boy and encourages Chibi to participate in the school pageant with an imitation of the voices of crows. After the performance, Mr. Isobe tells the other students that Chibi has walked many miles every day for six years to be able to attend class. The other children regret their previous treatment of Chibi and no longer make fun of him. At graduation, Chibi is the only student to win an award for perfect attendance. In later years, whenever he would come into town to get supplies for his family, the people in the village would greet him in a friendly manner, calling him Crow Boy, in memory of his wonderful school performance.

POSITIVE PARENTAL PARTICIPATION NOTE:

As parents, we are the first, and most important, mentors to our children. It is our job to build our children up by recognizing their unique qualities and praising them. Does your child love drawing? Encourage that gift by providing art supplies and a place to doodle. Take your child to art museums and exhibitions. Frame his work, hanging some of it in the house and giving some of it to beloved family members. Is your child a whiz at memorizing? When you go shopping, tell him several items on the list and check them off when he reminds you to purchase them. Allow him to help you prepare meals and, after you are done, encourage him to tell you the ingredients used. It is by positively interacting with our children that we help build their self-esteem.

CRAFTING:
BLACK AND WHITE PAINTING

Although Crow Boy had a difficult time expressing himself verbally, he was able to do so more easily with his artwork. Painting with various mediums (finger painting, water colors, sponge painting, etc.) was a very popular activity with my day care group, as well as with my own children and my kindergarten classes. You can help your child express himself artistically with this project.

You will need: Paper to paint on (construction paper or paper grocery bags cut open), black and white non-toxic tempera paint, brushes (or Q-tips), and cover-ups to protect the work surface and your clothing.

1. Cover the work surface and your clothing to protect from splatters.
2. Pour a small amount of black and white paint into two separate containers.
3. Let your child paint several pictures using different size brushes and/or Q-tips.

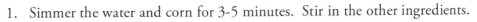

COOKING:
MISO SOUP

You will need: 4 cups water, 1 cup corn kernels, ½ cup chopped green onion tops, ¼ cup dark miso, 1 Tb honey, 1 Tb sesame oil, 1 sheet of nori seaweed (torn into small pieces), ¼ lb tofu sliced into long thin strips, and a large pot.

1. Simmer the water and corn for 3-5 minutes. Stir in the other ingredients.
2. Heat and serve. Serves 5.

READING:
ZARA'S HATS

Written and illustrated by Paul Meisel
(New York: Puffin Books, 2003)

Zara helps her parents decorate hats in the family hat shop. Disaster strikes when their supply of feathers is used up and they cannot obtain any more. Zara's father goes abroad to try to buy more feathers and, while he is away, Zara begins to decorate the untrimmed hats with fabric flowers and paper mache animals and fruits. Her hats are an immediate success and, when her father returns without any feathers, the hat shop continues to feature Zara's amazing hat creations.

POSITIVE PARENTAL PARTICIPATION NOTE:

What lessons can we learn from this story that can be implemented with our young children to help them develop a positive self-image? Zara and her parents participated in many activities together and, at a very young age, they allowed her to help in the hat shop. In addition, they encouraged her creativity and gave her positive feedback when she tried new ways of decorating the hats. Of course, we don't need to open a hat shop in order to build our children's self-esteem. By focusing on their special gifts and talents, we can make our children feel special at home every day!

NOTES:

_____

_____

_____

_____

_____

_____

_____

CRAFTING:
HAT-MAKING

You will need: 1 circle of felt material (about 12 inches across), ribbons, buttons, silk flowers and/or other items to adorn your hat, paste, and scissors.

1. Cut a hole in the center of the felt circle to fit your child's head.
2. Arrange the ribbons, buttons, silk flowers, etc. and paste in place.

COOKING:
CHILD-FRIENDLY DREAMY FRUIT SALAD

Zara used fruits to decorate her hats. You and your child can use some of the same fruits in this delicious salad…wonderful as a dessert that provides healthful fruit as the main ingredient.

You will need: 1 large package vanilla instant pudding, 1½ cups milk, 1 diced apple, 1 peeled navel orange, 2 bananas (sliced), ½ cup blueberries, ½ cup sliced strawberries and a large bowl.

1. Mix instant pudding and milk in a large bowl. Chill for 10 minutes.
2. Add diced apple, orange sections, bananas, strawberries and blueberries and mix together gently.
3. Makes 4-6 servings. Store leftovers in an airtight container in the refrigerator.
4. Creative tip: use your imagination and substitute different fruits.

READING:
THE FIVE CHINESE BROTHERS

Written and illustrated by Claire Bishop and Kurt Wiese
(USA: Coward-McCann, Inc. 1938)

In this old Chinese tale, we meet five brothers who look exactly the same, but each has a unique quality that sets him apart from the others. When one of the brothers inadvertently causes the death of a village child, the townspeople decide to kill him by cutting off his head. He asks if he can go home to say goodbye to his mother and, when permission is granted, he goes home and the brother with the iron neck goes back in his place. Of course, his head cannot be cut off, so the townspeople decide to drown him. Again he asks for permission to go home to say goodbye to his mother and, when he gets there, the brother whose legs can stretch to any length goes back in his stead. When the townspeople throw this brother in the water, he stretches his legs and keeps his head above the water. This process continues as each brother uses his unique gift to escape death. The townspeople decide that since the accused man can't be killed, he must be innocent and they let him go.

POSITIVE PARENTAL PARTICIPATION NOTE:

Each one of us has special gifts and talents that make us unique individuals. Children develop positive self-images when their gifts are recognized and encouraged.

NOTES:

_____

_____

_____

_____

_____

_____

_____

CRAFTING:
FISH MOBILE

Mobiles are fun to make and calming to watch as air currents move them gently.

You will need: A clothing hanger, construction paper, thread, yarn or ribbon, scissors, and markers.

1. Draw several different sized fish on construction paper and cut them out.
2. Decorate the fish with markers. Choose the two biggest fish and poke a small hole in the top and bottom, threading an 8-inch-long piece of thread, yarn or ribbon through each hole.
3. Attach the top threads to each end of the wire hanger. Attach the smaller fish to the bottom threads. When you hang up the mobile, the fish will move and twirl in the breeze.

COOKING:
CHILD-FRIENDLY TUNA BURGERS

Tuna salad is an old stand-by. Here is a clever way to use tuna in a different way for the ever-popular burgers!

You will need: 1 7-oz can tuna (drained), ½ cup chopped celery, ½ cup diced cheese (American or Cheddar), ¼ cup minced onion, ¼ cup mayonnaise, a small amount of margarine, 6 hamburger buns, aluminum foil, a baking sheet, and a bowl.

1. Mix the tuna, celery, cheese, onion and mayonnaise.
2. If desired, spread margarine on buns. Fill buns with tuna mixture.
3. Wrap each bun in foil and place on a baking sheet in the oven at 350 degrees for 15 minutes.
4. Serves 6. Open the foil packet and let the tuna burger cool a little before serving to your child.

READING:
SPAGHETTI EDDIE

Written by Ryan SanAngelo
Illustrated by Jackie Urbanovic
(Honesdales, PA: Boyds Mills Press, Inc., 2002)

Eddie loves to eat spaghetti, morning, noon and night. When his mother sends him to the store to buy frosting for his father's birthday cake, Eddie takes his bowl of spaghetti and meatballs along. He uses it in extremely creative ways: as a shoelace for a neighbor's shoe, to construct a fishing net for a friend, in place of guitar strings for someone's broken guitar. Eddie's use of his spaghetti and meatball lunch rises to heroic proportions when he knocks down a fleeing robber with a well-aimed meatball.

POSITIVE PARENTAL PARTICIPATION NOTE:

We all have unique qualities, as well as likes and dislikes. How fortunate for Eddie that his parents were understanding and supportive of his "spaghetti fixation". Whether your child wants to have spaghetti or some other food on a regular basis or refuses to eat some other item on his plate, try to work with him…it may be a short-lived stage and there are always creative ways you can use to introduce other foods. Participating with your child in the cooking experience and allowing him to help with other meal preparation will often encourage a "fussy" eater to try new foods.

NOTES:

_____

_____

_____

_____

_____

CRAFTING:
PASTA COVERED TREASURE BOX

Your child can make this for himself or as a gift for a loved one.

You will need: An empty cigar-type box (those are hard to come by these days, but you could substitute any small box or margarine-type container that has a lid), paste, and different types of dry pasta, especially colorful varieties.

1. Spread the paste on the outside of the container. Cover the entire surface with pasta shapes, pressing gently. Set aside to dry.
2. Spread paste on the top of the lid. Cover with pasta and allow it to dry.

COOKING:
CHILD-FRIENDLY SPAGHETTI AND MEATBALLS

You will need: For the meatballs: 1 lb lean ground beef (or ground chicken or turkey), 1 envelope dry onion soup mix, ½ cup grape jelly, 1 10-oz can of diced tomatoes, a mixing bowl, and a baking dish. For the spaghetti: 1 lb dry pasta...your child's favorite, and a large pot of boiling water. Optional: grated Parmesan cheese, 1 Tb olive oil.

1. Combine the ground beef and soup mix and form small walnut-sized balls. Place in the baking dish and bake at 350 degrees for 15 to 20 minutes. Drain off any fat.
2. Blend the jelly and diced tomatoes and pour over meatballs. Bake an additional 15 minutes.
3. While meatballs are baking, boil water in a large pot and add the spaghetti (or other pasta). Cook according to package directions and then drain.
4. Toss the spaghetti with a little olive oil if desired; serve on plates, topping each portion of pasta with meatballs, sauce, and some grated Parmesan cheese.
5. Serves 4-6, depending on appetites.

READING:
NORMAN THE DOORMAN

Written and illustrated by Don Freeman
(New York: The Viking Press, 1959)

Norman, the mouse, has a very important job at the art museum. He is the doorman at a small hidden hole in the wall and he gives tours of the basement art relics to visiting mice. He loves to express himself artistically, and when the art museum has a contest, Norman enters a wire sculpture made from a mousetrap. Norman's entry wins first prize and the museum guard gives him a tour of the entire building and a big chunk of cheese to enjoy with his friends later.

POSITIVE PARENTAL PARTICIPATION NOTE:

Norman was a very special mouse...and he knew it. He was extremely proud of the conscientious job he did as the doorman and guide to his mouse friends. In addition, he worked hard at his hobby...creating many beautiful works of art. We can help our children develop a sense of pride in themselves and their accomplishments by giving them opportunities to succeed as well as fail...by recognizing and praising their strengths, and also by encouraging and helping them to confront and overcome their weaknesses.

NOTES:

_____

_____

_____

_____

_____

_____

_____

_____

_____

CRAFTING:
WIRE SCULPTURE

Children enjoy working in many different art mediums...here is something a little different.

You will need: A piece of foam (from left-over packaging) or a lump of clay, some picture hanging wire, wire cutters or strong scissors (these are for the adult to use), and washers, beads and/or metal nuts.

1. Cut several lengths of wire (make sure the ends are not sharp or ragged).
2. Press one end of one piece of wire into the foam or lump of clay that will be the base for this project. Let your child twist and turn the wire, adding washers, beads and/or metal nuts for artistic design.
3. When he is finished with that wire, let him press the loose end into the base.
4. Continue with other pieces of wire until his wire sculpture is finished.

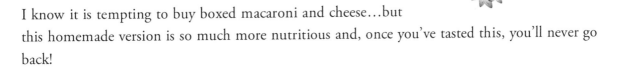

COOKING:
CHILD-FRIENDLY MACARONI AND CHEESE

I know it is tempting to buy boxed macaroni and cheese...but this homemade version is so much more nutritious and, once you've tasted this, you'll never go back!

You will need: 8-oz of macaroni, ¼ lb of cheddar cheese cut in pieces, 2 Tb of margarine, 2 cups of milk, a large pot, and a 9 by 13 inch lightly greased baking pan.

1. Cook the macaroni according to package directions.
2. Put the milk, margarine and cheese in a pot and heat on medium-low, stirring often until the cheese melts.
3. Pour over the drained macaroni and stir.
4. Put the mixture in the baking pan and bake at 350 degrees for 30 minutes until the top is golden brown.
5. Serves 4...just add a crisp green salad on the side.

READING:
BEWARE OF BOYS

Written and illustrated by Tony Blundell
(New York: Greenwillow Books, 1991)

A little boy goes walking through the woods and is kidnapped by a wolf. Although the wolf intends to eat him, the clever child suggests that the wolf prepare him according to a particular recipe and he instructs the wolf to get many different ingredients. Each time the wolf returns, the boy sends him to get additional items. This continues until the wolf collapses from exhaustion and the child is able to escape.

POSITIVE PARENTAL PARTICIPATION NOTE:

Although the story may seem quite silly and ridiculous, young children will admire the cleverness of the little boy and his ability to calmly assess the situation in which he found himself. We must help our young children develop the ability to stay calm and think things through, whether they are working on a difficult project or find themselves separated from the adult caring for them. There are various games you can play with your child that will encourage that type of decision-making. Of course, praising your child helps him believe in himself.

NOTES:

_____

_____

_____

_____

_____

_____

_____

_____

_____

_____

CRAFTING:
DECISION-MAKING GAME

You can make your own game board that includes many of the decisions a young child has to make in the course of his early years. You will need: A large piece of cardboard, colored markers, index cards, a pen, a set of dice, and several game pieces (different colored buttons would be great).

1. Draw a roadway on the cardboard, marking one end as the start and the other end as the finish and divide it into sections at even intervals.
2. Mark "pick a card" or "rest area" or "roll the dice again" on each section.
3. On the front of each index card, write a question such as "If you broke a toy at your friend's house, what would you do?" or "If you were at the mall with your family and couldn't find them, who could help you?" On the reverse side of the card, write an appropriate answer. Create at least one dozen cards.
4. Each player takes turns rolling the die, moving their button to the correct space on the roadway, and following the instructions of the section on which they land.

COOKING:
CHILD-FRIENDLY PUREE OF VEGETABLE SOUP

Let your child add one ingredient at a time to the big pot (before you put the pot on the stove)…just as the boy instructed…use your imagination…you can add other vegetables as well. *You will need: 2 large carrots (chopped), 1 stalk celery (chopped), 2 large potatoes (cubed), 3 cups water or vegetable broth, 1 medium onion (chopped), 1 tsp minced garlic, ¼ tsp thyme, ½ tsp salt, yogurt (optional), a large pot and a blender.*

1. Combine all ingredients (except salt and yogurt) in a large pot and boil.
2. Reduce the heat, cover and simmer for 45 minutes.
3. Puree the mixture in a blender until smooth and add salt if desired.
4. Garnish each serving with a Tb of yogurt. Makes 4 to 6 servings.

READING:
FREDERICK

Written and illustrated by Leo Lionni
(New York: Alfred A. Knopf, 1967)

During the fall, a mouse family scurries around to collect seeds and nuts for the winter. One mouse, however, does not seem to be doing anything except daydreaming. Frederick explains that he is collecting sunshine, colors and words, but his family believes he is just trying to avoid the "hard" work. When winter comes and the long cold days and nights seem endless, Frederick entertains his family and lifts their spirits by reciting the poetry he composed while the other mice were collecting seeds and nuts.

POSITIVE PARENTAL PARTICIPATION NOTE:

Each one of us has special gifts and, as a parent, you need to recognize and encourage your child's strengths and talents. Sometimes this is very difficult, especially if your child does not enjoy doing what the rest of the family likes to do. For example, most of the members of a family might love participating in all kinds of sporting activities, but one child in the family does not, preferring to draw or play a musical instrument. In a situation like this, it is even more essential for the parents to provide opportunities for that child to develop his own gifts and pursue his particular interests.

NOTES:

_____
_____
_____
_____
_____
_____
_____
_____

CRAFTING:
MAKE A BOUQUET OF COLORFUL PAPER FLOWERS

You will need: Construction paper in several colors, pipe cleaners, masking tape, a green marker, and scissors.

1. Cut a piece of construction paper (about 2 inches wide and 6 inches long).
2. Make 1-inch deep cuts along the paper and roll the cut side around a pencil for a minute. Remove the pencil and then wind the paper around the top of the pipe cleaner, cut side facing up…the curled paper will resemble flower petals.
3. Arrange the flowers in a small vase for a beautiful bouquet!

COOKING:
CHILD-FRIENDLY NUT BUTTERS

Why purchase processed peanut butter (or other nut butters) when you can easily make your own, without adding sugar, salt and preservatives.

You will need: A food processor or blender that can chop nuts, ½ lb peanuts (or any other nuts such as almonds, cashews or pecans).

1. Put the nuts in the food processor or blender. Cover and process until the nuts are finely ground. Add a few drops of canola oil, if desired.
2. Spoon out your nut butter and store in an airtight container.
3. Spread on bread, crackers, celery, apple slices…be creative!

READING:
MISS HUNNICUTT'S HAT

Written by Jeff Brumbeau
Illustrated by Gail De Marcken
(New York: Orchard Books, 2003)

When the Queen decides to pass through the town of Littleton, Miss Hunnicutt decides to wear a very special hat. Although everyone else in the town wants Miss Hunnicutt to take off her hat that has a live chicken on top because they think the Queen will be offended by it, Miss Hunnicutt refuses and maintains that she has a right to wear the hat of her choice. It turns out that the Queen has a hat with a live turkey on top. She asks Miss Hunnicutt to trade hats with her and come to a party at the palace. Miss Hunnicutt agrees and, in the days and weeks that follow, many of the townspeople come to appreciate Miss Hunnicutt for who she is and they begin wearing hats decorated with chickens.

POSITIVE PARENTAL PARTICIPATION NOTE:

Assertiveness is a very valuable trait and parents need to encourage their children to develop it…by allowing your child to express his individuality, you teach him that you value his special qualities and his ideas. Of course, we want our children to listen to us and obey us, especially when it comes to safety issues such as holding our hand when they cross the street. However, whenever possible, we need to let our young children follow pursuits of their own choosing.

NOTES:

_____

_____

_____

_____

_____

_____

_____

CRAFTING:
HAT MAKING

You will need: A paper sack to fit your child's head, ribbons, buttons, silk flowers, and/or small pictures (from magazines or old greeting cards), paste, and scissors.

1. Open the bag and cut up along the four edges (about 1-2 inches).
2. Fold up the front, back and sides for the brim (you can cut the brim for a fringe-like effect).
3. Choose ribbons, buttons, pictures and/or flowers and paste all over the bag for a decorative hat, just like Miss Hunnicutt had.
4. Take a picture of your child in his hat and display it in your home.

COOKING:
CHILD-FRIENDLY STRAWBERRY YOGURT PIE

The perfect dessert…delicious and full of healthful ingredients!

You will need: 1 cup plain yogurt, 1 8-oz package softened cream cheese, 2 Tb honey, 1 tsp vanilla, 1 8-inch graham cracker pie crust, 2 cups of strawberries and a large bowl.

1. Wash and hull strawberries. Set aside 8 of the nicest ones and cut the rest in half.
2. In a large bowl, combine yogurt, cream cheese, honey, and vanilla and beat with a wooden spoon until smooth.
3. Pour half of this mixture into the prepared crust.
4. Top with the halved strawberries and cover with the rest of the yogurt mix.
5. Arrange the 8 reserved strawberries on top of the pie.
6. Chill in the refrigerator for 6 hours or until firm.

NOTES:

CHAPTER THREE: "I LOVE YOU AND YOU LOVE ME!"

How to help your child feel appreciated, loved and accepted

"**I wanna** go see Mickey Mouse! I wanna go see Mickey!" wailed four-year old Andrew as he watched a commercial for Disneyland on the television. "Mollie and Becca went with their mommy and daddy, and Tommy went with his granny. Everyone is going away except me," he cried. Andrew's mother turned off the television and sat down next to him on the well-worn couch. "We don't have the money to go on that kind of vacation," she told him, hugging him tightly. "But, we can go on a special vacation to the park, just like the two little girls did in a story I got from the library. As soon as you put away your toys, you can help me make some sandwiches and we can read the story while we have a picnic in the park." Andrew quickly started picking up his puzzle pieces and blocks, while his mother put *Mimmy and Sophie* by Miriam Cohen in a small canvas shopping bag and then added cold juice boxes and some fruit. After helping his mother make tuna salad sandwiches, Andrew sat at the kitchen table, drawing designs and pictures on brown paper lunch bags, while his mother cut and wrapped the sandwiches that would go into them. As they left the apartment, Andrew held his mother's hand, skipping happily in anticipation of his special vacation.

> *"Being loved and lovable, valued and valuable as we are, regardless of what we do, is the beginning of the most fundamental kind of self-esteem." Gloria Steinem*

POSITIVE PARENTAL PARTICIPATION NOTE:

Children who value themselves have a self-confidence that helps them become involved in life. The main characters in each of the stories in this chapter are helped to feel appreciated, loved and accepted by the significant adults in their lives and, by reading each story and participating in the accompanying art activity and cooking experience, you will be able to help your children develop a positive self-image as well.

READING:
THE DO-SOMETHING DAY

Written and illustrated by Joe Lasker
(New York: The Viking Press, 1982)

Bernie decides to run away because his family is too busy to pay attention to him and do things with him. As Bernie passes through his small town, various shopkeepers ask for his help and they each give the little boy something to thank him for helping them. He hands salamis to the butcher, feeds the fish for the owner of the pet shop and waters the produce vendor's horse. When Bernie returns home, his family is very happy to see him and he shares all of the gifts that he received. Each member of Bernie's family expresses their appreciation for the gifts and tells Bernie how much they need him. This helps Bernie feel loved and valued.

POSITIVE PARENTAL PARTICIPATION NOTE:

Young children can be very demanding of their parents' time, and it often seems that there is not enough time to do everything we need to accomplish. However, we must show our children that we value and appreciate them…and the best way to do that is to spend some "quality" time with them. Whether we are reading them a story, or working on a craft project, or baking a batch of cookies, "positive parental participation" comes into play…that is, we need to set aside that special time and really "be" with our children, whole-heartedly enjoying this precious time with them.

NOTES:

_____

_____

_____

_____

_____

_____

_____

CRAFTING:
MAKE A ROAD MAP

You and your child can decide whether you want to make a map of your street or, perhaps, a main street of your town or city.

You will need: Large piece of cardboard, colored markers, old magazines, scissors, and paste.

1. Walk with your child on the street you have decided to map and make a rough sketch (on a piece of scrap paper) of where the various homes or stores will be.
2. Transfer the information onto the cardboard.
3. Cut pictures of houses, stores, trees, etc. from magazines and paste in the appropriate places on your road map.

COOKING:
CHILD-FRIENDLY RYE BREAD

You will need: 2 Tb dark brown sugar, 2 Tb margarine, 1 Tb salt, 1 cup boiling water, ½ cup cold water, ½ cup warm water, 1 package active dry yeast, 2½ cups rye flour, 3 cups white flour, large and small bowls, baking sheet, and a little corn meal.

1. Mix sugar, margarine, salt and boiling water in small bowl and add cold water.
2. In large bowl, combine warm water with yeast and stir to dissolve.
3. Beat in sugar mixture and rye flour. Add 2½ cups white flour gradually.
4. Continue to add white flour until dough is fairly stiff and knead on floured surface 8-10 minutes. Shape into ball, place in greased large bowl (turning to grease all sides), cover with clean cloth and let rise till doubled (about 1½ hours).
5. Punch down, knead lightly, divide dough in half and shape each into round loaf.
6. Place on corn meal sprinkled baking sheet, cover and let rise till doubled (1 hr).
7. Bake 30 to 35 minutes at 400 degrees till brown. Cool on wire rack.

READING:
THE STORY OF FERDINAND

Written by Munro Leaf
Illustrated by Robert Lawson
(New York: The Viking Press, 1936)

Long ago in Spain, a young bull named Ferdinand loved to sit under the shade of a tree and smell the flowers. Even though the other bulls would race around, fighting with each other and butting heads, Ferdinand only wanted to sit and smell the flowers. When some men came to pick the biggest and fiercest bull to fight in Madrid's famous bullring, Ferdinand was chosen because when he sat on a bee, the sting made him jump around like crazy and the men were impressed with his strength and energy. In the bullring, however, Ferdinand noticed the flowers of the ladies in the audience and he sat down in the middle of the ring to enjoy the smell. No matter what the men did, they could not make Ferdinand move, so they brought him back to his field where he could sit under his favorite tree and smell the flowers.

POSITIVE PARENTAL PARTICIPATION NOTE:

Each one of us is a unique individual. We can help our children develop high self-esteem by recognizing, accepting, and enthusiastically encouraging their individuality.

NOTES:

_____

_____

_____

_____

_____

_____

_____

_____

CRAFTING:
DAISY CHAIN NECKLACE

You will need: Several sheets of construction paper (yellow and white), length of ribbon, paste, scissors, package of ziti pasta, small piece of tape, and a hole puncher.

1. Cut out at least a dozen white daisy shapes. Also cut small yellow circles for the center of each flower. Paste the yellow circles in the middle of the white daisies.
2. Punch a hole in the middle of each daisy. Wrap a piece of tape around one end of the ribbon so you can push it through the hole easily.
3. Tie a ziti on the other end of the ribbon and start stringing daisies and pieces of ziti alternately.
4. If you wish, you can use non-toxic tempera paint or a marker to color the ziti green before you begin this project (make sure they are dry before you begin putting them on the ribbon)…they will look like the stems of the daisies.

COOKING:
CHILD-FRIENDLY BAKED SPANISH RICE

You will need: ½ cup minced onion, 2 Tb canola oil, ½ cup minced green pepper, ½ cup uncooked rice, ¼ tsp chili powder (optional), 1 lb can tomatoes, ½ cup water, 1 bay leaf, ¼ tsp sugar, ½ cup grated Cheddar cheese, a large pan, and a casserole dish.

1. In a large pan, heat oil to medium and lightly brown onion and green pepper.
2. Add the rice and stir for a minute or two.
3. Transfer to casserole dish and add remaining ingredients.
4. Mix lightly, cover with aluminum foil and bake for 30 minutes at 350 degrees.
5. Uncover and bake for 5 more minutes.
6. Serves 4 as a main dish or 6-8 as a side dish.

READING:
WILLIAM'S DOLL

Written by Charlotte Zolotow
Illustrated by William Pene Du Bois
(USA: HarperCollins Publishers, 1972)

William wants a doll to take care of and to love, but his father and older brother make fun of him because they only want him to enjoy playing with trains and basketballs. Although William does enjoy those pursuits, he still wants to have a doll. Fortunately, his understanding grandmother comes to visit. She takes him to the toy store and buys him the very doll he has been wanting. When William's father complains, she explains that having a doll to nurture will help prepare William to be a wonderful father one day.

POSITIVE PARENTAL PARTICIPATION NOTE:

Each person is a unique individual and each child must be valued, loved and accepted for who he is. As parents, we must refrain from judging our children… we must love them whether they are short or tall, blue-eyed or brown-eyed, serious or always laughing. In addition, we must encourage them to pursue their own creative paths and stop trying to push them into any preconceived patterns we have for them.

NOTES:

_____
_____
_____
_____
_____
_____
_____
_____
_____

CRAFTING:
SOCK DOLL

You will need: One clean sock, clean pantyhose (or other socks) for stuffing, handful of dried beans, 12 inch piece of ribbon, small pieces of felt, buttons, needle and thread, paste, and scissors.

1. Cut the sock just above the heel and push stuffing into the sock (the toe will be the head). Add a handful of beans for weight and sew the open end completely closed.
2. To form the neck, gently squeeze the sock just below the toe and tie the ribbon.
3. From small pieces of felt, cut feet, hands, nose, mouth and eyes and paste onto the doll's head and body. You can attach buttons for an added decoration.
4. You can add some stitches to the felt features and buttons to make sure they don't fall off.

COOKING:
CHILD-FRIENDLY CURRIED VEGETABLE MEDLEY

Measure all the vegetables with your child…she can draw designs on construction paper to make special placemats to use with this meal while you add the ingredients to the pan.

You will need: 1 cup yogurt, 1 tsp margarine, ½ cup chopped onion, ½ cup diced celery, 1 cup broccoli, 1 cup cauliflower, 1 cup diced potatoes, 1 cup thinly sliced carrots, ¼ cup chopped green pepper, ¼ cup raisins, ¼ cup chopped apples, 1 cup apple juice, ½ tsp curry paste or curry powder, and a large saucepan with cover.

1. Melt margarine in pan and add curry, onion and celery and stir well.
2. Add remaining ingredients (except yogurt), stir well and bring to a boil.
3. Lower the heat to simmer, cover pan and cook until potatoes are tender (about an hour) stirring occasionally.
4. Add the yogurt, stir to blend, heat through and serve with basmati rice.
5. Serves 2-3 as a main dish and 4-6 as a side dish. Store in an airtight container in the refrigerator up to three days.

READING:
YOU'RE ALL MY FAVORITES

Written by Sam McBratney
Illustrated by Anita Jeram
(Cambridge, MA: Candlewick Press, 2004)

Three young bears pose two very important questions to their parents…are we the most wonderful baby bears in the world and which of us is your favorite? Fortunately, Mother Bear and Father Bear are able to give their curious children satisfactory answers to both queries.

POSITIVE PARENTAL PARTICIPATION NOTE:

Young children often wonder the same things even though they may not verbalize their thoughts. Spending time with your child and treating his ideas and opinions with respect are two important ways a parent can help a child feel valued, loved and accepted. And, as this story shows, telling your child how proud you are of him and how wonderful he is certainly helps build that all-important positive self-image.

NOTES:

_____

_____

_____

_____

_____

_____

_____

_____

_____

_____

_____

CRAFTING:
FUR-COVERED BEAN BAG BEARS

You will need: For each bean bag: A piece of faux fur material about 6x6 inches, several buttons, ½ cup dried beans or rice, scissors, a needle and some thread.

1. Fold the material in half (fur-side in) and draw a bear shape.
2. Cut out and sew along the edges, leaving the top of the head area open.
3. Turn right side out and fill with beans or rice.
4. Sew the top of the head area closed. Sew on buttons for eyes and nose.
5. Important tip: The cutting and sewing will probably have to be done by the parent…but your child will love filling the beanbag with beans. If you have a sewing machine, you could do several and then play a beanbag toss game with your child.

COOKING:
CHILD-FRIENDLY MINI BEAR CLAWS

You will need: 2 eggs, ½ cup canola oil, ½ cup sugar, 1 tsp baking powder, ½ tsp almond flavor, 2½ to 3½ cups flour, 1½ cups diced apples, ¼ cup raisins, ¼ tsp cinnamon, a large bowl, rolling pin, large round cookie cutter, and a lightly greased cookie sheet.

1. Combine all ingredients, (except apples, cinnamon and raisins), adding the flour gradually, to make soft dough.
2. Divide dough into 3 balls. Roll out the first ball on a floured surface.
3. Cut out circles with a cookie cutter or a wide mouth jar.
4. Mix the apples, cinnamon and raisins together and put a spoonful of this filling in center of each circle and fold over, pressing the edges together.
5. Make several cuts with scissors along the straight edge of the filled dough and place on a lightly greased cookie sheet. Save the extra scraps of dough and re-roll them together to cut out more circles.
6. Repeat with the other balls of dough and bake at 325 degrees for 20-30 minutes or until edges are lightly browned.
7. Makes about 18 to 20 mini-bear claws.

READING:
THE UGLY DUCKLING

Written by Hans Christian Anderson
Illustrated by Robert Ingpen
Translated by Anthea Bell
(New York: Penguin Young Readers Group, 2005)

Although the original story was written almost two hundred years ago, there have been hundreds of editions of this beloved classic fairy tale because its message is timeless. A mother duck hatches a misplaced swan's egg and, although the baby bird that emerges seems big and clumsy compared to the other cute little ducklings, the mother duck recognizes his superior swimming ability. Unfortunately, the other barnyard animals are extremely unkind and the young bird leaves his home to escape the abuse. He has many adventures on his journey and several times comes close to losing his life during the harsh winter. He continues to believe that he is ugly and useless until the spring arrives and he sees three elegant swans swimming on a beautiful pond. The other swans greet him lovingly and, after looking at his reflection in the water, he discovers that he has grown up and is a beautiful swan as well.

POSITIVE PARENTAL PARTICIPATION NOTE:

When a person looks into the mirror, he sees himself with his mind's eye... a combination of his actual physical appearance and how he believes others see him. Young children are particularly susceptible to the comments of parents (and others who provide care for them, as well as older siblings) and the things we say without thinking can have a tremendous impact. We must strive to speak positively with our young children, celebrating their "special-ness", while helping them to turn their weaknesses into strengths and their failures into successes.

CRAFTING:
ORIGAMI BIRDS

You will need: 3-inch or 4-inch square of thin paper (copy paper is fine, construction paper might be too thick) and a marker.

1. Fold the square of paper in half to form a triangle.
2. Fold the top corner down so the point extends past the baseline of the triangle.
3. Lift up the top flap of the point. This is the head. Then fold the triangle in half.
4. Fold back each wing halfway. Add eyes, beak and feathers with the marker.

COOKING:
CHILD-FRIENDLY ENGLISH MUFFIN BREAD

You will need: 2 packages dry yeast, 1 tsp salt, 1 Tb sugar, 2 cups lukewarm water, 5 cups flour, 1 Tb cornmeal, a large bowl, and a greased baking sheet.

1. In a large bowl, mix the yeast, salt, sugar and water.
2. Add 4½ cups flour, 1 cup at a time, mixing well.
3. Remove the dough from the bowl and knead for 5 minutes on a floured surface, adding more flour if necessary to make the dough firm.
4. Place the dough in a clean greased bowl, cover with a cloth and let rise for 1 hour.
5. Punch down and shape into 2 loaves.
6. Place on a baking sheet sprinkled with cornmeal. Slash the tops with a knife. Brush with water and let rise 15 minutes.
7. Place the baking sheet in a cold oven, set temperature to 400 degrees and bake 45 minutes. Remove and cool loaves on a wire rack.

READING:
GUESS HOW MUCH I LOVE YOU

Written by Sam McBratney
Illustrated by Anita Jeram
(Cambridge, MA: Candlewick Press, 1994)

Little Nutbrown Hare is ready for bed and begins to tell Big Nutbrown Hare how much he loves his father. He stretches his arms as high as he can and says he loves his father as high as he can reach. His father responds by stretching his arms as high as he can reach (which, of course, is much higher) and he tells his son that he loves him that much. This conversation continues and the father continues to reassure his son of the abundant love he feels for him. Little Nutbrown Hare drifts off to sleep, secure in the knowledge of his father's love.

POSITIVE PARENTAL PARTICIPATION NOTE:

As parents, we try to make sure that our young children have good food to eat, warm clothes to wear, and a safe place to live. To develop a healthy self-image, food for the mind is just as important. A child needs to know he is loved, valued and accepted for who he is. You will not spoil your child because you tell him you love him every day of his life.

NOTES:

_____
_____
_____
_____
_____
_____
_____
_____
_____
_____

CRAFTING:
MILK-CARTON RABBITS

You will need: 2 milk cartons (one-quart size and one-pint size), non-toxic tempera paint (mixed with a little laundry detergent so the paint will stick to the wax-coated cartons), construction paper, paste, scissors, cotton balls, and pipe cleaners.

1. Paint the cartons and let them dry.
2. Cut out eyes, ears, mouth and paws from construction paper. Stand each carton up and paste the construction paper features in their proper places.
3. Paste a cotton ball at the back of each carton for the "cottontail" and attach a few pipe cleaners above the mouths for each nose.

COOKING:
CHILD-FRIENDLY NUTBROWN SALAD

This lovely dish can be served with dinner or lunch…but it is sweet enough to use for dessert, as well (something like an applesauce made of carrots)…a nice take-along for summer picnics, too!

You will need: 1 lb of carrots (peeled and grated), 4 ounces of crushed pineapple packed in juice, ½ cup of slivered almonds (optional), ¼ cup flaked coconut, ½ cup sour cream (or yogurt), ¼ cup raisins, and a large bowl.

1. Mix all ingredients in a large bowl.
2. Chill in refrigerator.
3. Store in airtight container in fridge. Use within a few days.
4. Makes about 3 cups.

READING:
THE TALE OF PETER RABBIT

Written by Beatrix Potter
Illustrated by Allen Atkinson
(New York: Alfred Knopf, 1988)

There are scores of editions of this beloved classic, but the story remains the same. Peter Rabbit lives with his mother and sisters and brothers in a rabbit hole under a big tree. Although his mother cautions him to be good and go with his siblings to pick blackberries, Peter cannot resist the temptation to investigate Farmer MacGregor's garden. Once there, he helps himself to various vegetables, and is soon discovered by the farmer. He narrowly escapes, losing his jacket and shoes. The upset stomach he has from eating too many vegetables prevents him from enjoying the delicious dinner his mother had prepared.

POSITIVE PARENTAL PARTICIPATION NOTE:

Although Peter disobeyed his mother, she continued to treat him with loving kindness. Sometimes it is very difficult to love someone who disobeys and does not listen to our counsel. However, as parents, we must continue to love our children, no matter what, even when we do not love their behavior.

NOTES:

_____
_____
_____
_____
_____
_____
_____
_____

CRAFTING:
STACKING RABBITS

You will need: Dinner and snack sized paper plates, scissors, a stapler, construction paper, paste, and a marker.

1. Cut the paper dinner plate in half, overlap the ends and staple together.
2. Cut out bunny ears from construction paper and glue on either side near the point.
3. Cut out eyes and paws from construction paper and attach. Use the marker to add other features.
4. Repeat steps 1-3 with the smaller plate. Each plate can be used to make two rabbits so your child can make an entire rabbit family!

COOKING:
CHILD-FRIENDLY MARINATED VEGETABLE SALAD

This recipe makes a dish that is delicious and healthful...perhaps your child will love this "vegetable salad" as much as Peter Rabbit did.

You will need: 2 cups of cauliflower, 2 cups of carrots (scraped and cut into thin sticks), 1 small bunch of broccoli, 1 onion (peeled and sliced thin), ½ cup vegetable oil, 2 Tb balsamic vinegar, 2 Tb prepared mustard, and a saucepan.

1. Separate cauliflower and broccoli into flowerets; combine with carrot sticks and onions in a saucepan with ½ inch of boiling water.
2. Cover and simmer 5 minutes and then drain and cool.
3. Mix oil, vinegar and mustard and pour over drained vegetables.
4. Serves 2-3 as a main dish, 4-6 as a side dish. Serve hot or cold.
5. Store in an airtight container in the refrigerator for up to one week.

READING:
YOU'RE JUST WHAT I NEED

Written by Ruth Krauss
Illustrated by Julia Noonen
(USA: HarperCollins Publishers, 1998)
(Text originally published in 1951)

Discovering a bundle under the blanket on her bed, a young mother teasingly guesses what it could be, listing several funny and improbable things that she doesn't need (such as a load of laundry and a monkey). Her little daughter finally reveals herself to her mother who lovingly embraces her and states that her daughter is just what she needs.

POSITIVE PARENTAL PARTICIPATION NOTE:

Young children want to feel needed and valued. Our children are special gifts to us and we must treasure them. Don't hesitate to tell your child on a daily basis how much you love him…his self-esteem grows each time!

NOTES:

_____

_____

_____

_____

_____

_____

_____

_____

_____

_____

CRAFTING:
APPLIQUE A BLANKET THROW

You can help your child make a personalized blanket throw for his bed. Let him choose the color for the throw and then talk about what pictures he would like to appliqué on it...perhaps your child is a sports enthusiast and would like to appliqué a basketball, baseball, football, etc. If your child loves animals, he might want to appliqué a cat, dog, rabbit, etc.

You will need: A large rectangle of felt or flannel (about 1 yard by 2 yards), several pieces of felt or other material for the appliqués, scissors, paste, and a marker.

1. After your child decides the theme for the appliqués, you can help him draw the figures on the smaller pieces of material or you can find suitable pictures in magazines and trace them onto the material.
2. Cut out the figures, balls, animals, etc. Arrange on the large piece of felt or flannel and then paste in place. If you want to insure that the figures don't fall off, you could add some needle and thread stitching.

COOKING:
CHILD-FRIENDLY PEANUT BUTTER COOKIES

You will need: ½ cup canola oil, ½ cup honey, ¾ cup peanut butter, 2 eggs (beaten), ½ cup instant dry milk, 1 tsp baking powder, 1 tsp cinnamon, ½ cup quick rolled oats, ½ cup raisins, 1½ cups whole wheat flour, a large bowl, an electric mixer, and a lightly greased baking sheet.

1. In a large bowl, beat oil and honey with the electric mixer.
2. Beat in peanut butter, eggs, dry milk, baking powder and cinnamon.
3. With a wooden spoon, mix in oats, raisins and flour.
4. Drop by teaspoonfuls onto baking sheet.
5. Bake at 325 degrees for 10 to 12 minutes.
6. Makes about 30 cookies. Store in airtight container.

READING:
I LOVE YOU BECAUSE YOU'RE YOU

Written by Liza Baker
Illustrated by David McPhail
(New York: Scholastic Cartwheel Books, 2001)

Mother Fox tells her son that she loves him when he is happy as well as when he is angry, when he is sick in bed as well as when he is running around, when he is shouting as well as when he is quiet. Little Fox, of course, is very comforted by the fact that his mother loves him just as he is.

POSITIVE PARENTAL PARTICIPATION NOTE:

Young children need to know that we will love them no matter what. This level of unconditional love and acceptance will encourage them to come to us with their problems and concerns. It will also enable them to show love to others and develop healthy relationships with others, now and throughout their lives.

NOTES:

_____

_____

_____

_____

_____

_____

_____

_____

_____

_____

_____

CRAFTING:
LOVE COLLAGE

You will need: A piece of construction paper, old magazines, scissors, paste, and a marker.

1. Talk to your child about the things he loves…his family, his pets, playing ball, eating ice cream, the color blue, etc.
2. Look through the magazines and help your child cut out pictures that epitomize what he loves.
3. Paste the pictures onto the paper…let your child use the marker to draw additional things (or people) he loves that he couldn't find pictures of, such as himself and you!

COOKING:
CHILD-FRIENDLY SESAME DROPS

Here is a sweet treat that contains high-quality nutrition!

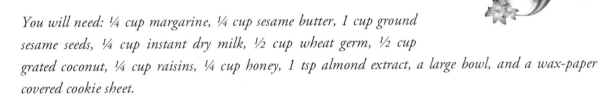

You will need: ¼ cup margarine, ¼ cup sesame butter, 1 cup ground sesame seeds, ¼ cup instant dry milk, ½ cup wheat germ, ½ cup grated coconut, ¼ cup raisins, ¼ cup honey, 1 tsp almond extract, a large bowl, and a wax-paper covered cookie sheet.

1. Cream together the margarine and the sesame butter.
2. Blend in the remaining ingredients except for the grated coconut.
3. Form 1-inch sized balls; roll each in the grated coconut and place on the cookie sheet.
4. Chill in the refrigerator for several hours.
5. Store in an airtight container in the refrigerator.
6. Makes about 18 walnut-sized pieces. Since these nutritious treats are very filling, you might want to make smaller ones for younger children.

READING:
I LOVE YOU WITH ALL MY HEART

Written by Noris Kern

Adapted and illustrated by Jean Baptiste Baronian

(San Francisco: Chronicle Books, 1998)

Polo, the baby polar bear, wonders what it means when his young caribou friend, Walter, tells him that his mother loves him with all her heart. Polo goes home to ask his mother and she explains that she loves him with her mouth when she kisses him, with her paws when she tickles him, with her belly when she hugs him: in other words, with her whole self or whole heart. Polo is extremely comforted by this revelation, and before he goes to sleep, he tells his mother that he loves her with all his heart, also.

POSITIVE PARENTAL PARTICIPATION NOTE:

Young children need to be reassured that their parents love them. All too often, we interact with our children only when we want to correct their behavior. This is really a reinforcement of their negative behavior. Instead, I would suggest the principle of Positive Parental Participation. If you are enjoying the time you spend with your young child, whether it is reading the picture book or working on the crafting project or cooking experience, that joyful interaction will help your child feel valued and valuable, an important step in the formation of high self-esteem.

NOTES:

_____

_____

_____

_____

_____

_____

_____

CRAFTING:
STORY BOOK OF LOVE

You will need: A small notebook or several sheets of construction paper stapled along the left edge, old magazines, scissors, paste, and markers.

1. Talk to your child about the people and things he loves…family members, ice cream cones, walks in the park, riding his bike, and, hopefully, himself.
2. Help him find pictures in magazines that correspond to what he has mentioned and cut out and paste them onto the pages of the "story book of love". Or, he can draw the pictures himself.
3. At the bottom of each page, write your child's words.

Important tip: At another time, make your own "story book of love" to show to your child…make sure your love for him figures prominently on at least one of the pages.

COOKING:
CHILD-FRIENDLY HEARTS OF MOZZARELLA SALAD

You will need: 1 chunk of mozzarella cheese (about 1 lb), 2 Roma tomatoes, 1 Tb basil (dry or fresh), several leaves of romaine lettuce, 1 Tb balsamic vinegar, 1 Tb olive oil, and 1 Tb Parmesan cheese.

1. Cut mozzarella into 8 slices (¼ inch thick). Use a heart shaped cookie cutter or a knife to cut each slice into a heart shape (put the excess cheese in a plastic bag in the fridge to save for topping on pizza, etc.).
2. Slice each tomato into 4 slices and place a tomato slice on top of each cheese heart.
3. Arrange on a platter of lettuce leaves and sprinkle each serving with olive oil, balsamic vinegar, basil and Parmesan cheese.

READING:
LITTLE GORILLA

Written and illustrated by Ruth Bornstein
(New York: Clarion Books, 1976)

Everyone in the jungle loves Little Gorilla. Giraffe helps him when he is stuck in a tree, and Elephant cools him off with a shower. His parents and extended family tell Little Gorilla that they love him very much. As Little Gorilla grows up, he gets bigger and bigger, and, although his size is somewhat intimidating, his animal friends still love him and accept him.

POSITIVE PARENTAL PARTICIPATION NOTE:

New babies almost always seem to get an outpouring of love and attention. However, as they grow up, young children often feel they don't "measure up" to the expectations of their parents who sometimes neglect to express their love for their young children as much as they did when their children were babies. We need to let our children know how much we value them and accept them for who they are, not who we want them to be.

NOTES:

_____

_____

_____

_____

_____

_____

_____

_____

_____

_____

CRAFTING:
BIG AND LITTLE ANIMAL COLLAGE

You will need: A piece of construction paper, old magazines, scissors, paste, and markers or crayons.

1. Help your child find animal pictures in old magazines. If possible, find a large and small of each type. Cut out the pictures.
2. Paste the pictures on the paper…if you weren't able to find two different sizes, you or your child can draw the larger (or smaller) animal.

COOKING:
CHILD-FRIENDLY APPLE CAKE

The wonderful aroma of apples and cinnamon baking in the oven…you and your child will have smiles on your faces all day long!

You will need: 2 cups all purpose flour, ½ tsp salt, 1 tsp baking soda, 1 tsp ground cinnamon, 1 cup sugar, ¾ cup canola oil, 2 eggs beaten, 2½ cups apples (peeled and sliced thinly), ½ cup applesauce, ½ cup raisins, a large bowl, a 9x13-inch greased baking pan, and a spatula.

1. In a large bowl, mix the flour, salt, baking soda, cinnamon and ¾ cup sugar.
2. Make a well in the center of the flour and add the oil and eggs. Mix well.
3. Add the apples and raisins and stir until well distributed.
4. Spread the batter in the pan. Smooth with a spatula and sprinkle with ¼ cup sugar.
5. Bake at 350 degrees for 35 to 45 minutes.
6. Insert a toothpick in the center of the cake…the cake is done if it comes out clean.
7. Serve warm or at room temperature. Serves 12.
8. Refrigerate leftovers in an airtight container.

READING:
DAVID GETS IN TROUBLE

Written and illustrated by David Shannon
(New York: Blue Sky Press, 2002)

David always seems to be doing or saying something wrong…he breaks a window while playing baseball, he goes to school without his pants on, he pulls the cat's tail, he makes silly faces for the school class picture, and he eats the dog's biscuits. His excuses are as varied as his mishaps. Although his mother punishes him for his misbehavior…time outs in the corner, soap in his mouth, early bedtime…it is obvious (to the reader and to David) that she loves him, no matter what!

POSITIVE PARENTAL PARTICIPATION NOTE:

Young children need to know that they are loved, even when they misbehave. Parents need to express, in both word and deed, how much they love, value, and accept their young children, regardless of their behavior.

NOTES:

_____

_____

_____

_____

_____

_____

_____

_____

_____

_____

CRAFTING:
FLOATING SOAP BOATS

Although David's mother used soap as a somewhat questionable disciplinary measure, here is a much more enjoyable way to use a bar of soap! *You will need: 1 bar of Ivory soap, several pipe cleaners, a piece of construction paper, scissors, string, and crayons.*

1. Soak a bar of floating soap in warm water to soften it a little. Then take it out and dry it off.
2. Push three pipe cleaners into the top of the soap where the name is (the middle one should be the highest) and one pipe cleaner on an angle into the narrow end of the soap.
3. Cut 3 small rectangles and 1 small triangle from construction paper and decorate with stripes, zigzags or other designs. Make two small holes in each paper shape and slide onto the pipe cleaners…these are the ship's flags.
4. Tie the string from stick to stick until all four sticks are connected.

Important tip: If you and your child make several, he will have a fleet of ships to play with in the tub…just make sure you check for pipe cleaners, string or flags before you let the water out of the tub to insure nothing but water and soapsuds go down the drain.

COOKING:
CHILD-FRIENDLY EGG IN A NEST

You will need: For each serving: 1 slice of whole wheat bread, 1 Tb margarine, 1 egg, several sprigs of parsley, a non-stick skillet and a 2½ inch round cookie cutter.

1. Spread both sides of bread with margarine and cut out center. If you don't have a cookie cutter, you can use a knife to carefully cut a large circle from the center of the bread.
2. In the skillet on medium low, lightly brown one side of bread and the cut out center. Remove the circular center of bread and save.
3. Break the egg into hole in the bread slice, cover the pan and cook on low about 3 minutes. Flip it over to cook the other side.
4. Transfer to a plate and top with the reserved circular center of the bread. Garnish with sprigs of parsley to imitate tree branches.

READING:
WILL YOU STILL LOVE ME?

Written by Jean Baptiste Baronian
Illustrated by Nora Kern
(San Francisco, CA: Chronicle Books, 2001)

Little Polo wonders why his polar bear parents seem to be too busy to play with him. He is sure it is because they don't love him anymore and he goes to ask his friends. They advise him to talk to his parents about how he feels. Polo does and he discovers that his mother is going to have a baby and, more importantly, that his parents will always love him.

POSITIVE PARENTAL PARTICIPATION NOTE:

Young children often blame themselves when parents argue or have marital problems. They are sure that if they were smarter or better, everyone would be happy. In addition, they rarely understand that parents have enough love no matter how many children there are. Parents need to reassure their children by what they say and by how they act that there is, indeed, enough love to go around.

NOTES:

_____
_____
_____
_____
_____
_____
_____
_____
_____
_____

CRAFTING:
SOAP SUDS SNOW POLAR BEAR

Polo, the polar bear, comes from the arctic regions of our world where snow and ice are constant companions. You and your child can make "snow" even in the summer and, depending on the consistency, you can use it like clay to mold into shapes or like frosting to cover other surfaces. For this project you will use it like clay. *You will need: 2 cups of packaged soap flakes (like Ivory), water, an eggbeater or electric mixer, cover-ups for the work surface, and a bowl.*

1. Cover your work surface. Pour 2 cups of soap flakes and ½ cup water into a large bowl and whip with beater or mixer, adding soap flakes if necessary until the batter is a doughy consistency…you may have to use a wooden spoon near the end of the mixing.
2. Dip your hands in water so the "dough" doesn't stick to you…take a portion of the flake mixture and mold into a small ball (the head). Do the same with more of the mixture and make a larger ball (the body). Add small amounts for the ears, snout, tail, arms and feet…attaching by moistening with water.
3. Use small buttons for eyes. This little polar bear will harden and last for weeks. If you wish, remove the buttons and then your child can use it to wash with.

COOKING:
CHILD-FRIENDLY COCONUT COVERED
LEMON BON BONS

Here are more snowballs…edible, that is!

You will need: ¾ cup butter or margarine, 1 cup flour, ½ cup cornstarch, ½ cup powdered sugar, 1 tsp lemon rind, a package of shredded coconut, a large bowl, and a lightly greased cookie sheet.

1. Mix all of the ingredients except the coconut. Chill 15 minutes and then roll into balls.
2. Roll each ball in the coconut and place on greased cookie sheet. Press down gently with a fork or the bottom of a glass.
3. Bake at 300 degrees for 20 minutes. Remove carefully to cool on a wire rack.
4. Makes about 24 cookies. Store in airtight container.

READING:
OLIVER BUTTON IS A SISSY

Written and illustrated by Tomie de Paola
(New York: Harcourt Brace Jovanovich, 1979)

Oliver Button enjoys walking in the woods, reading books, drawing pictures and, most of all, dancing. His father tries to convince him to play baseball or football, but Oliver is firm about his likes and dislikes. Although the boys tease him at school and call him a sissy, Oliver continues to pursue the activities he enjoys. When he performs in a talent show and his classmates watch him dance, they come to see him in a more favorable light.

POSITIVE PARENTAL PARTICIPATION NOTE:

How can we give our young children a sense of pride? Although Oliver's father would have preferred that he participate in sports like the other boys, he was willing to encourage his son in his chosen pursuits. When Oliver's father allowed Oliver to take dance lessons and then went to the talent show to see his son perform and praised him for his dancing, he helped Oliver feel good about himself. We can help our young children develop a positive self-image in the same way.

NOTES:

_____
_____
_____
_____
_____
_____
_____
_____
_____
_____
_____

CRAFTING:
ACTIVITY COLLAGE

You will need: Construction paper, old magazines, scissors, and paste.

1. Look through old magazines with your child and help him find pictures of people engaged in various activities (gardening, dancing, sports, etc.).
2. Cut out the pictures and paste them on the construction paper.
3. Let your child tell you which activities he enjoys and which he dislikes.

COOKING:
CHILD-FRIENDLY ENGLISH MUFFIN PIZZA

This easy recipe was a great favorite in our home…for lunch, dinner or as a nutritious snack.

You will need: For each serving: 1 English muffin, 2 Tb of your favorite tomato pasta sauce (or you can substitute canned or fresh diced tomatoes, chopped green pepper, and/or chopped onion), 1 tsp grated Parmesan cheese, 1 Tb shredded mozzarella cheese, and a cookie sheet.

1. Split the muffin and top each half with 1 Tb sauce (or fresh veggies), ½ tsp Parmesan cheese and ½ Tb mozzarella cheese.
2. Place the muffins on the cookie sheet and bake about 10 minutes at 350 degrees, until the cheese is melted and the sauce is bubbly.
3. Let the muffins cool slightly before serving to young children (be careful…the sauce under the melted cheese can be VERY hot).

Important tip: You can add toppings before baking such as: sliced mushrooms, diced green pepper, chopped onions, broccoli florets, strips of cooked turkey or chicken breast…use your imagination!

READING:
A DIFFICULT DAY

Written and illustrated by Eugenie Fernandes
(Toronto, Ontario: Kids Can Press, 1987)

Melinda does not get a good night's sleep and the next day is filled with unpleasant moments. When her mother insists that the little girl take a bath, Melinda complains, but, when her mother says it is time to get out of the tub, Melinda throws a temper tantrum and is sent to her room. She hides under her bed and feels that nobody loves her. Meanwhile, Melinda's mother realizes that her daughter is having a bad day and brings milk and freshly baked cookies to share with her. When her mother cannot find her, Melinda calls to her mother and they both express their love for each other and share the milk and cookies under the bed.

POSITIVE PARENTAL PARTICIPATION NOTE:

We all have "bad" days when nothing seems to go right. At times like these, young children often feel unloved. I have found that when a child's behavior makes him seem unlovable, that is when he most needs to be reassured that he is loved. Parents need to provide daily confirmation of their love for their children... by what they say and by what they do.

NOTES:

_____

_____

_____

_____

_____

_____

_____

_____

CRAFTING:
"YOU ARE A STAR" NECKLACE

You will need: A package of sticky stars and a piece of ribbon about 25 to 30 inches long.

1. Measure the ribbon so that it fits comfortably around your child's neck when the ends are tied in a bow.
2. Lay the ribbon flat on the work surface.
3. Let your child choose the stars he wants on his necklace (all the same color or variegated) and help him gently press each star onto the middle five inches of the ribbon. If the ribbon is wide enough you will only need stars on one side. However, if the ribbon is very narrow, you may have to turn the ribbon over and cover each sticky star with a matching star so that the sticky side doesn't stick to your child's neck.
4. Help your child put his necklace on…he is a star…today and every day!

COOKING:
CHILD-FRIENDLY OLD FASHIONED MOLASSES GINGER COOKIE STARS

You will need: ½ cup canola oil, 1 cup molasses, 2 Tb warm water, 1 egg (well beaten), 3 cups flour, ¼ tsp salt, ¼ tsp baking soda, ½ tsp ginger, 1½ tsp cinnamon, 2 large bowls, a greased cookie sheet, a rolling pin, and star-shaped cookie cutters.

1. Mix together the butter, molasses and warm water and then add the beaten egg.
2. Add the remaining ingredients to the mixture. (You will have a soft dough)
3. Let it stand for 15 minutes and then roll it out on floured surface until ¼ inch thick.
4. Cut with star cutters and place on the cookie sheet.
5. Bake at 375 degrees for about 15 minutes. Makes about four-dozen cookies.
6. Store in an airtight container. These are very crispy cookies…if you roll the dough to about ½ inch thickness, the cookies will be a little chewier.

READING:
MOMMY DOESN'T KNOW MY NAME

Written by Suzanne Williams
Illustrated by Andrew Shachat
(Boston: Houghton Mifflin Company, 1990)

Hannah's mother has many different names of endearment that she uses for her little daughter, and Hannah imagines herself as each one: chickadee, pumpkin, monkey, etc. Throughout the day we see how involved Hannah's mother is with her: they have breakfast together, she takes her daughter to a friend's house to play, and, in the evening, they listen to music and dance together. At bedtime, Hannah's mother reassures her of the love she has for her daughter. We can see by the expression on Hannah's face that the little girl is truly confident of her mother's love and acceptance of her, no matter how she behaves.

POSITIVE PARENTAL PARTICIPATION NOTE:

The illustrations in this book help us to see how imaginative young children are. It is wise to remember that little ones are easily frightened and always believe what their parents tell them (at least when they are very young). We want our children to trust us and believe that we love, value and accept them. Therefore, we need to be honest with them and refrain from threatening them with punishments we would never carry out. How often have you heard a parent tell a misbehaving child, "I'll kill you when we get home" or "I'm leaving you now if you don't come this minute"? These invectives are worse than useless because at first they frighten the child who may believe his parent will hurt him or abandon him. Then, when this empty threat is not carried out, the child realizes that his parent says things he doesn't mean...so when that parent says "I love you", perhaps he doesn't mean that either.

CRAFTING:
BOOKPLATES

From infancy on, my children owned their own books…I still have several of the original ones that were reread hundreds of times. These small treasuries of wonder and knowledge helped create individuals who love to read and who were able to use books to expand their insight into the nature of the world and themselves. You can help your child create his own bookplates to proclaim his ownership of these precious treasures.

You will need: White paper, old magazines, fine line marker, scissors, and tape.

1. Help your child choose and cut out several favorite pictures from the magazines (about 2 or 3 inches square in size). Paste each onto a piece of paper 4 inches square and write your child's name at the bottom and carefully tape one onto the inside front cover of your child's book.
2. Do this for each of your child's books.

COOKING:
CHILD-FRIENDLY GOOD MORNING SHAKE

Fruit shakes and smoothies are quite nutritious…especially if you use fresh organic ingredients…perfect with breakfast or lunch or as a refreshing snack.

You will need: 2 oranges (peeled and sectioned…make sure there are no pits), 1 frozen banana sliced, ¼ cup orange juice, 2 Tb yogurt, ½ tsp vanilla, and a blender.

1. Put all ingredients into the blender and blend until smooth.
2. Pour into glasses and garnish with a small orange slice on the rim of the glass, if desired.
3. Makes 8-10 ounces, depending on the size of the oranges.

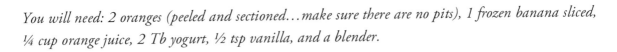

READING:
NOBODY NOTICES MINERVA

Written and illustrated by Wednesday Kirwan
(New York: Sterling Publishing Co, Inc., 2007)

Poor Minerva! Her older brother and her baby sister seem to get all the attention, so Minerva decides to do some naughty things like poke her brother with a fork and pick all of the leaves off her mother's plant. Her father speaks very kindly to her and explains that she is very special to him, but that perhaps she would like to be noticed for other behaviors. Minerva helps her brother set the table and reads a story to her baby sister and, enjoying the wonderful praise she gets from her parents, Minerva resolves to be noticed for good behavior.

POSITIVE PARENTAL PARTICIPATION NOTE:

When young children exhibit negative behavior, they are usually sending out a cry for attention or help. Parents need to let their children know, on a daily basis, that they are loved and valued. We should not wait until a child is misbehaving to notice what he is doing…why not notice when your child has picked up a toy without being asked to do so, or has amused himself for a short period of time while you were busy on the phone.

NOTES:

_____

_____

_____

_____

_____

_____

_____

_____

_____

_____

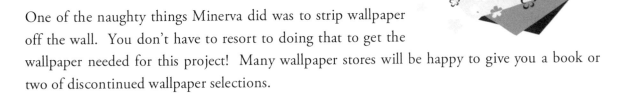

CRAFTING:
WALLPAPER MOSAIC

One of the naughty things Minerva did was to strip wallpaper off the wall. You don't have to resort to doing that to get the wallpaper needed for this project! Many wallpaper stores will be happy to give you a book or two of discontinued wallpaper selections.

You will need: Several small sheets of wallpaper, a piece of cardboard, paste, scissors, and a marker.

1. Cut or tear the sheets of wallpaper into small pieces (about 1 inch x 1 inch).
2. Your child can draw a design on the cardboard and then paste the small pieces of wallpaper into each section of the design.

COOKING:
CHILD-FRIENDLY BREAKFAST OATMEAL

Minerva and her family were having oatmeal for breakfast...very healthful and very delicious. We always used steel cut oats...they have a nutty flavor and a more hardy texture than rolled or quick oats. You and your family can enjoy some as well.

You will need: 1½ cups water, 1½ cups milk, ¼ tsp salt, 1 tsp margarine, 1 cup steel cut oats, a pot with a cover, and maple syrup or honey.

1. Bring the water, milk, oats, and margarine to a boil in a pot.
2. Turn the burner to low and cover. Cook 10 to 20 minutes on low, stirring occasionally.
3. Remove from the heat and serve with a little milk, a pinch of salt and a spoonful of maple syrup or honey, if desired.
4. Serves 4.

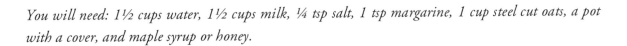

READING:
MIMMY AND SOPHIE: THE VACATION

Written by Miriam Cohen
Illustrated by Thomas Yezerski
(New York: Farrar, Straus and Giroux, 1999)

Summer is coming and all the children are boasting about where they are going for vacation. Mimmy and Sophie don't have anything to contribute to the discussion because their parents are struggling financially. When Mimmy and Sophie ask their parents if they can take a vacation somewhere, their mother suggests they have a special picnic on the Brooklyn Bridge. After helping their mother make egg salad sandwiches, the two little girls accompany their parents to the store where they buy a special treat…cupcakes with filling. Mimmy and Sophie enjoy the picnic on the bridge and spend the rest of the afternoon watching the boats in the river and the beautiful sunset. Although they have not traveled far, both girls are satisfied with the wonderful day they have spent with their parents.

Positive Parental Participation Note:

Mimmy and Sophie were fortunate because their parents were sensitive to the needs and concerns of their children. They used their imagination to plan a wonderful afternoon for their daughters and, with very little money, enabled Mimmy and Sophie to enjoy a very special vacation. The time their parents spent with them helped Mimmy and Sophie understand how much they were loved. As parents, we need to listen to our children and spend time with them just like the parents in the story…Positive Parental Participation in action!

Notes:

_____

_____

_____

_____

CRAFTING:
WATERCOLOR WASH SUNSET PAINTING

Watch the sunset with your child the day before you do this project.

You will need: A piece of painting paper or white construction paper, non-toxic tempera paints (red, orange, yellow, blue), brushes or Q-tips, small bowls, and crayons.

1. Let your child draw a picture on the paper with crayons.
2. Pour several drops of blue paint into a small bowl and add some water, a little at a time, mixing with the brush or Q-tip. Apply the wash to the entire picture.
3. In another bowl, do the same thing with the red paint and apply this wash to the upper area of the picture. Repeat with the yellow paint and then with the orange paint until your child is satisfied with his sunset.

COOKING:
CHILD-FRIENDLY EGG SALAD SANDWICHES

You will need: For two sandwiches: 2 hard boiled eggs, mayonnaise or salad dressing to taste, 4 slices of whole wheat bread, lettuce, tomato and/or sprouts.

1. Put two fresh eggs in cold water and bring to boil. Lower the heat and simmer for 5 minutes. Turn off heat and let eggs sit in hot water for 5 more minutes.
2. Remove eggs and run under cold water. Carefully remove the shells.
3. Mash the eggs in a bowl and add mayonnaise or salad dressing. Mix until smooth.
4. Spread on piece of bread or toast, cover with another piece of bread and slice.
5. Garnish your sandwiches (and add nutrition) with lettuce, tomato and/or sprouts.

Notes:

CHAPTER FOUR: "I AM REALLY MAD RIGHT NOW!"

How to help your child express his feelings

I stood in the doorway of the bathroom, staring at the letter "P" penciled on the toilet seat. Four-year old Peter was having a hard time finding his place in the family between his bright seven-year old brother and his adorable new baby sister and was involved in one mischievous situation after another. I picked up *Where The Wild Things Are* by Maurice Sendak and went to find Peter who was building a fort in the playroom. He came to me immediately when I sat down in the story chair. "Are we going to read a story?" Peter asked. I set him on my lap and we read about the night Max

> *"When we are safe enough to bounce our feelings back and forth without fear of harm, then we shall have peace."*
> Tori Ugunda

did a lot of naughty things and was sent to bed without any dinner. "Will I have to go to bed without any dinner?" Peter queried. Tears rolled down his face as he added, "I was writing my name on paper. I went to the bathroom and I was feeling mad that Jason is big and Caroline is little and I am not big enough or little enough." Hugging my son, I replied, "Everyone feels sad or mad sometimes. If you talk about how you feel, we can try to help you feel better." Peter looked up at me with a smile as I said, "We love you just the way you are. You are just the right size to make your own book to read at family story-time. But first we have to clean the toilet seat." Peter slid off my lap, relieved that I had acknowledged his feelings in a positive way. Skipping ahead, Peter replied joyfully, "I can help, Mommy!"

POSITIVE PARENTAL PARTICIPATION NOTE:

Emotions are a part of being human, and learning to express them in positive ways is a lifelong task that begins in childhood. We need to help children identify how they are feeling, we need to accept those feelings, and we must teach our children how to express their feelings in a constructive manner. In this chapter, you will find picture books that focus on anger, frustration, jealousy, envy, happiness and sadness. You can help your child's self-image grow as he learns how to acknowledge his feelings and express them in constructive ways.

READING:
AND MY MEAN OLD MOTHER WILL BE SORRY, BLACKBOARD BEAR

Written and illustrated by Martha Alexander
(Cambridge, MA: Candlewick Press, 1969)

Anthony's mother gets angry when Anthony makes a mess while he is taking a bath. While she is cleaning up the bathroom, Anthony makes an even bigger mess, spilling honey all over the kitchen. His mother loses her temper and yells at him to go to his room. Anthony loses his temper also, and decides to run away with the chalkboard bear that has come to life. After spending an uncomfortable (and somewhat scary) night in the woods, Anthony decides that he misses his mom and his home, and he returns to his room.

POSITIVE PARENTAL PARTICIPATION NOTE:

We all feel like running away sometimes. Life can be very difficult and we don't always see eye to eye with the ones we love. Creating an atmosphere of trust and acceptance will encourage your child to share his feelings with you, whether positive or negative. And, each time he shares his feelings with you and is not criticized, he is learning to value and accept himself. Of course, we would not expect Anthony's mother to be happy about the messes her son made, but it would have helped if she had conveyed the fact that even though she did not love what Anthony did, she still loved Anthony.

NOTES:

_____
_____
_____
_____
_____
_____
_____
_____

CRAFTING:
SIDEWALK CHALK

The chalk is a little messy to make (your child will love that), but lots of fun to use…clean up the pavement with a garden hose or bucket of water and a brush or broom.

You will need: 1 box Plaster of Paris, a large plastic bowl (disposable) and a stirrer to mix, tempera paint (liquid or powder), an empty toilet paper roll reinforced with duct tape all the way around the sides as well as over one end (a separate roll for each color) or, instead of the paper roll, you could use small paper cups.

1. Wear old clothes or cover-ups…mix a small amount of Plaster of Paris with water in the plastic container. The plaster should be stiff but creamy…add a little more water if necessary and then add a small amount of tempera paint…stir well and pour into the toilet paper roll or paper cup.
2. Let the chalk harden about 30 minutes…you can use it then or wait until it is completely dry (about 24 hours).

COOKING:
CHILD-FRIENDLY CREAMSICLE ICE POPS

As a child, my favorite treat when the ice-cream man arrived was always the orange sherbet and vanilla ice cream sensation called a creamsicle. Cool and refreshing, a little tart, a little sweet…make it with your child and see why I loved it so much. *You will need: 1 cup softened vanilla ice cream or ice milk, 1 cup orange sherbet, 1 (11 ounce) can of mandarin orange sections (drained), 6 small paper cups with Popsicle sticks or Popsicle molds, and a blender.*

1. Mix the ice cream (or ice milk), sherbet and drained orange sections in a blender.
2. Spoon into molds or paper cups and then freeze until firm. Insert Popsicle stick into each cup after 90 minutes if you wish or you can eat it straight out of the cup.
3. Makes 6 servings, about 3 ounces each. Best eaten within a few days.

Important tip: Experiment with different flavors of ice cream and other fruits!

READING:
FEELINGS

Written and illustrated by Aliki
(New York: Greenwillow Books, 1984)

Each page of this book is an examination into some of the feelings we all experience. In the corner of many of the pages, a baby bird makes comments to his mother about the scene that is unfolding. On one page we see an awesome space capsule, built of blocks, and all the children in the class are commenting on it. Most of the children are complimenting Tom, the little boy who built it. However, John, one of his classmates, has an angry expression on his face and says, "I could do that!" On the next page, the space capsule is destroyed and the children in the class are commiserating with Tom and yelling at John because he was the one who knocked the blocks down.

POSITIVE PARENTAL PARTICIPATION NOTE:

Young children will certainly identify with the scenarios pictured in this book, but I would suggest it be read in small increments...one story per sitting. In this way, you and your child will be able to talk about each scene and discuss how each of you would react in a similar situation. What a wonderful opportunity to examine just about every emotion a person could experience!

NOTES:

_____

_____

_____

_____

_____

_____

_____

CRAFTING:
HOW TO MAKE A SUNDIAL

In one of the stories, Alfred opens Bob's gift, a sundial. Here are instructions for making a sundial like Bob's...your child will enjoy telling time with it outside in the sun.

You will need: Two pieces of heavy cardboard, a drawing compass, a ruler, a pen, scissors, masking tape, a directional compass, and a watch or clock.

1. Cut one cardboard into a square (12 x 12 inches). Place the point of the drawing compass at the midpoint on one edge and draw a half circle from corner to corner.
2. Cut the other cardboard into a triangle (12 x 12 x 17 inches).
3. Tape the triangle upright across the center of the cardboard square so it divides the half circle in two and take the sundial outside in the sun. Place it so that the triangle points directly north (use your directional compass).
4. Keep track of the time with a watch and, at each hour, label that hour at the point on the half-circle where the shadow falls.

COOKING:
CHILD-FRIENDLY FROSTED BIRTHDAY CAKE

You will need: For the cake - ½ cup honey, ½ cup canola oil, 2 eggs, 2 tsp vanilla, ½ cup milk, 2 cups whole wheat flour, ½ cup soy flour, ½ cup non-fat dry milk, 2 tsp baking powder, 1 tsp cinnamon, 1½ cups mashed bananas, 2 large bowls, and a 9 x 13 inch pan. For the frosting you will need: 1 container whipped cream or make your own frosting by beating the following ingredients together: 2 Tb margarine, ¼ cup honey, 1 tsp vanilla, 2 Tb milk, 1 cup non-fat dry milk, and ¼ tsp cinnamon.

1. In one bowl, cream the honey and oil. Beat in the eggs, vanilla and liquid milk.
2. In another bowl, stir together all the dry cake ingredients. Add to the liquid ingredients and beat well. Stir in the mashed banana and beat well again.
3. Pour into the lightly greased pan and bake at 350 degrees for about 45 minutes.
4. Frost the cooled cake with whipped cream or your own frosting and decorate with blueberries or strawberries, if desired.

READING:
HURTY FEELINGS

Written by Helen Lester
Illustrated by Lynn Munsinger
(Boston: Houghton Mifflin Company, 2004)

Fragility was a hippopotamus who never cried if she hurt her toes, but always cried when her feelings were hurt…and she was so sensitive that her feelings were always getting hurt. When someone complimented her, she thought they were insulting her. Life was becoming very lonely for Fragility because everyone was afraid to talk to her. One day, during a soccer game, Fragility saw that others were sensitive as well, and this observation helped her to react more positively to what was being said to her.

POSITIVE PARENTAL PARTICIPATION NOTE:

The foundations for self-esteem are laid in the first five years of life and that is why it is so important to do everything possible to help our young children develop a positive self-image. Parents and others can inadvertently say things to children that are quite hurtful such as, "What a mess you've made! You're such a sloppy boy!" "Hurry up, slowpoke! We're always late because of you!" "Did you fall off your bike again? You'll never be good at anything!" Encourage your child to talk about the things that people say that hurt his feelings…he will realize that he is capable of hurting the feelings of others also.

NOTES:

_____

_____

_____

_____

_____

_____

_____

CRAFTING:
ANIMAL FLIPBOOK

A sense of humor is one of the most important character traits we can help our young children develop. This animal flipbook will have everyone giggling.

You will need: 4 sheets of construction paper, paste, scissors, 4 animal pictures (large enough to almost cover the page...if you can't find appropriate pictures in a magazine, you might have to draw them yourself), a hole-puncher, and a ribbon.

1. Punch three holes along the left side of each sheet of construction paper.
2. Thread the ribbon through each set of holes and tie securely to make a book.
3. Cut out the animal pictures and paste each on a separate page.
4. Cut the entire book in three sections from right to left, stopping about an inch before the left edge.
5. When you flip any section of each page, the animal will then have the head and/or body and/or legs of a different animal.
6. If you and your child enjoyed this project, try making a flipbook using pictures of people.

COOKING:
CHILD-FRIENDLY AMBROSIA SALAD

This salad was a favorite at picnics and potlucks when my children were small. In the story, Rudy the elephant went to eat a salad for lunch...perhaps it was this one!

You will need: 1 cup well-drained mandarin orange sections, 1 cup well-drained pineapple chunks, 1 cup flaked coconut, 1 cup vanilla yogurt, and a large mixing bowl.

1. Mix all of the ingredients in a large bowl.
2. Cover and chill at least an hour.
3. Serve as is or on lettuce leaves. Makes 4-5 servings. Can be stored in the refrigerator in an airtight container for several days.

READING:

I FEEL HAPPY AND SAD AND ANGRY AND GLAD

Written and illustrated by Mary Murphy
(New York: Dorling Kindersley Publishing, Inc., 2000)

Two little puppies, Milo and Ellie, experience many different emotions as they play together. At first they are happy, but when they play hide and go seek, Milo is puzzled because he can't find his friend. She makes a noise from the bush she is hiding in and Milo is scared, but when he realizes it is only Ellie, he feels glad. Trouble arises when Milo brings out his scooter and Ellie can ride it faster than Milo can…now Milo is angry and won't let Ellie ride it anymore. When Ellie goes home, Milo feels lonely and is ashamed of his behavior. The friendship is restored when Milo goes to see Ellie with his scooter and they ride on it together. Now everyone is happy!

POSITIVE PARENTAL PARTICIPATION NOTE:

Sometimes it is difficult to get along with others. Sharing possessions is a learned behavior. If you respect your child's ownership of his possessions, he will be more likely to share with others. The more confident your child is of his own worth and value, the easier it will be for him to accept and admire the worth and value of others. Encouraging your child to acknowledge and voice his feelings is an important step in this process.

NOTES:

_____

_____

_____

_____

_____

_____

CRAFTING:
PAPER PLATE FACES

We experience many different emotions…but there are two main categories of feelings, those that make you smile and those that make you frown. *You will need: 1 paper plate, crayons or markers, yarn for hair, buttons for eyes, paste, and scissors.*

1. On one side of the paper plate, help your child paste on buttons for eyes and yarn for hair and draw a big smile. Do the same on the other side, but draw a frown.
2. Pose various scenarios and let your child respond by holding up the happy or sad side of the plate to indicate how he would feel in that particular situation.

COOKING:
CHILD-FRIENDLY HAPPY FACE DOUBLE
APPLE PANCAKES

Pancakes were definitely a favorite breakfast for my children and I used raisins to create happy faces on each pancake. What a great way to start the day! *You will need: 1 cup sifted flour, ¼ tsp salt, 1 Tb sugar or honey, 2 tsp baking powder, 1 egg (lightly beaten), ¾ cup milk, 2 Tb canola oil, ¼ cup applesauce, 2 Tb chopped apple, ½ cup raisins or blueberries, maple syrup or warmed jelly for topping (optional), a non-stick griddle, and 2 bowls.*

1. Mix the flour, salt, sugar, and baking powder in a large bowl.
2. Combine the egg, milk, and oil in small bowl and then slowly stir the liquid mix into the dry ingredients and mix until just blended…the batter should be lumpy. Gently fold in applesauce and apples.
3. Preheat the griddle over moderate heat and pour or spoon the batter (about 2 or 3 Tb of batter for each pancake) onto griddle.
4. Cook until bubbles form over surface and turn gently to brown other side.
5. Press raisins or blueberries into surface of each pancake for eyes, nose and, of course, smiling mouth! Your child might enjoy arranging the faces on her own pancakes.

Top with warm maple syrup or jelly, if desired. Serves 4.

READING:
KISS IT BETTER

Written by Hiawyn Oram
Illustrated by Frederic Joos
(New York: Dutton Children's Books, 1999)

Whenever Little Bear is hurt or feeling sad, Big Bear is always there to give her a band-aid and a kiss. Although she loses her best friend, she finds a new best friend, and she learns that no matter how bad things may seem, we should always look toward the future with optimism. When Big Bear is sad, Little Bear helps to cheer him up by giving him lots of kisses and lots of band-aids.

POSITIVE PARENTAL PARTICIPATION NOTE:

Your child needs your love and your support...
just knowing that you are available for him to talk to, and that you won't criticize him for his feelings, will go a long way toward helping him deal with those feelings in a constructive manner. You will be teaching him to be caring and nurturing toward others as well.

NOTES:

_____
_____
_____
_____
_____
_____
_____
_____
_____
_____

CRAFTING:
HUGS AND KISSES COUPON BOOK

When our daughter was in the second grade, her gift to her father for his birthday was an envelope of handmade coupons, each good for one hug, to be used whenever he felt the need for some extra love. It was a gift that brought tears to our eyes, and it showed us that she had learned the importance of positive human interaction. I'm happy to say that although more than twenty years have passed since that birthday, Caroline is still the most loving and compassionate young woman I know. You can help your child make a coupon book that he can use when he feels the need to give or get an extra hug or kiss. *You will need: Several sheets plain white paper, 1 piece of construction paper folded in half (this will be the cover), crayons or markers, a stapler, and scissors.*

1. Let your child decorate the front cover of the coupon book.
2. Cut the sheets of white paper in half and write "Good for One Hug" on several and "Good for One Kiss" on some others and staple inside the cover.
3. Explain to your child that whenever he is feeling sad or in need of an extra hug or kiss, he can present the coupon to you. Make sure you let him know that he doesn't even need a coupon…all he needs to do is ask. *Important tip: When your child comes to you with one of the coupons, you will have a special opportunity to talk to him about whatever is on his mind.*

COOKING:

CHILD-FRIENDLY OATMEAL MINI-KISS COOKIES
You will need: 1 cup sifted flour, 2 tsp baking powder, ½ tsp salt, ½ cup margarine (soften to room temperature), 1 cup firmly packed light brown sugar, 1½ cups uncooked quick-cooking oatmeal, 2 eggs (lightly beaten), 1 tsp vanilla, 1 bag organic dark chocolate chips, 2 large bowls, greased baking sheets, and wire racks.

1. Mix the flour, baking powder and salt in one bowl.
2. Stir the margarine and sugar together in the other bowl until just mixed.
3. Blend in the flour mixture, oatmeal, eggs and vanilla.
4. Drop by rounded teaspoonfuls, 2 inches apart on greased baking sheets.
5. Gently press one or more chips into each mound of cookie dough.
6. Bake 15 to 18 minutes at 350 degrees until lightly browned…then cool on wire rack. Makes about 3½ dz. Store in airtight container.

READING:
JULIUS: THE BABY OF THE WORLD

Written and illustrated by Kevin Henkes
(New York: Greenwillow Books, 1990)

Lilly eagerly awaits the birth of her baby brother, but when Julius finally arrives, Lilly wishes that he would go away. Her jealousy causes her to resent the attention her mother and father shower on Julius, even though they continue to treat her with love and affection as well. She sings mean songs to him and pulls his little mouse-tail and spends a lot of time in the uncooperative chair. Lilly's attitude towards her baby brother finally undergoes a metamorphosis when her cousin insults Julius and Lilly defends her brother.

POSITIVE PARENTAL PARTICIPATION NOTE:

Lilly's parents try very hard to understand and support their daughter because they realize that even though they tell Lilly that they still love her, it is difficult for her to share their love and attention with her little brother. They listen to Lilly and punish her for her mean actions, not for how she is feeling.

NOTES:

_____

_____

_____

_____

_____

_____

_____

_____

_____

_____

CRAFTING:
POPSICLE STICK PUPPETS

Role-playing is a marvelous way to encourage young children to tell you about how they are feeling. Let your child put on a puppet show with his family of puppets...you can join in to help, perhaps taking the role of one of the children in the family and allowing your child to be the mother or father...then **listen carefully because you never know what you will learn.**

You will need: Several Popsicle sticks, construction paper, markers and/or crayons, magazines (optional), scissors, and paste.

1. Let your child decide how many puppets he wants to make and who they will be.
2. Have him draw the people or use pictures from the magazines.
3. Cut out the people and paste them onto the top half of each Popsicle stick.
4. Put on a play!

COOKING:
CHILD-FRIENDLY NUTTY APPLESAUCE PARTY CUPCAKES

Young children love to (and need to) feel special...have your child help you make these healthful, high nutrition party cupcakes and then have a tea party, just like Lilly did. It can be a party for just your child and you (and perhaps several favorite stuffed animals) or a party with some of your child's friends.

You will need: 1 cup applesauce, ½ cup honey, ¼ cup canola oil, 1¼ cup whole wheat flour, ¼ cup soy flour, 1 tsp baking soda, 1 tsp cinnamon, ½ cup ground peanuts or almonds, ½ cup hulled sunflower seeds, 1 can whipped cream or 1 container cream cheese, 2 mixing bowls, an electric mixer, lightly oiled muffin tins, and a wire rack.

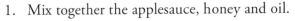

1. Mix together the applesauce, honey and oil.
2. Combine the dry ingredients and mix into the wet ingredients.
3. Stir in the nuts and seeds and fill each muffin cup about ¾ full.
4. Bake at 350 degrees for about 15-20 minutes until golden.
5. Cool on a wire rack and then top with whipped cream or cream cheese.
6. Make 12 muffins. Store in an airtight container.

READING:
TODAY I FEEL SILLY & OTHER MOODS THAT MAKE MY DAY

Written by Jamie Lee Curtis
Illustrated by Laura Cornell
(New York: Joanna Cotler Books, 1998)

From one day to the next, the main character shares her moods with us and tells us why she is feeling silly or mad or glad. Happiness, anger, joy, confusion and excitement are some of the other emotions she experiences. At the end of the book, she tells us that although she prefers having positive feelings, she realizes that whatever her emotional state is, it is OK to feel that way.

POSITIVE PARENTAL PARTICIPATION NOTE:

Your child needs to acknowledge and accept the many feelings she has...and as a parent, you need to accept those feelings as well, whether they are positive or negative ones. When you show your child that you love her, no matter how she is feeling, you validate her worth as a person. This validation will help your child develop a positive self-image.

NOTES:

_____

_____

_____

_____

_____

_____

_____

_____

_____

CRAFTING:
DECORATE A DRESS-UP STORAGE BOX

Sometimes it is difficult for young children to tell us how they are feeling. Dressing up in silly or fancy clothes allows a child to be someone else for a moment…and in that disguise, she may be able to talk about what is on her mind. We always had a box of all kinds of clothing that the children could use as costumes…let the show begin!

You will need: 1 large strong cardboard box (to hold the clothes), markers or crayons, an assortment of buttons and/or a box of multi-colored pasta, ribbon, paste, and scissors.

1. Let your child draw pictures and/or designs on the sides of the box.
2. Now paste on buttons and/or pasta shapes and pieces of ribbon.
3. Fill the box with discarded hats, ties, shawls, long skirts, necklaces, earrings, etc. Tip: You might want to keep the jewelry in a separate plastic container.
4. Dress up with your child and have a hot cocoa party.

Another tip: If you don't have suitable clothing for the dress-up box, visit your local Goodwill store for inexpensive treasures.

COOKING:
CHILD-FRIENDLY BLUEBERRY SHERBET

You will need: 2 cups frozen blueberries, ¼ cup yogurt, ½ Tb honey, ¼ cup apple juice, and a blender.

1. Blend together: blueberries, yogurt and juice.
2. Add the honey and blend until smooth and creamy.
3. Spoon into container and freeze for about 30 minutes.
4. Makes about 1 cup of sorbet. Best eaten within 2 or 3 days.

Important tip: You can experiment with different fruits (such as strawberries or watermelon), different flavor yogurts, and different varieties of juice.

READING:
WHERE THE WILD THINGS ARE

Written and illustrated by Maurice Sendak
(New York: HarperCollins Publishers, 1963)

When Max chases after his pet dog with a fork and bangs nails into the wall with a hammer, he is sent to his room without having had dinner. He dreams that he sails to the land of the wild things where he is made king. However, he misses his family and returns home to find his dinner waiting for him in his room…and it is still warm.

POSITIVE PARENTAL PARTICIPATION NOTE:

Young children get into mischief, sometimes because they are sad or mad or upset about something that they have trouble talking about. Perhaps they have a new baby brother or sister, or the adults in the family are not getting along, or there is a bully at nursery school. When you encourage your child to come to you with his problems, and you listen without judging, he will feel comfortable expressing his emotions, whether they are positive or negative.

NOTES:

_____
_____
_____
_____
_____
_____
_____
_____
_____
_____
_____

CRAFTING:
MY OWN PICTURE BOOK

How proud your child will be to see his own storybook on the shelf! I still have several books that my children made when they were very young. You can help your child make his very own picture book. You will be encouraging his love of books and helping build his self-esteem at the very same time. *You will need: Several sheets of construction paper, old magazines, scissors, paste, a hole-puncher, ribbon, and a pen or marker.*

1. Talk to your child about his book…what would he like it to be about?
2. Fold several sheets of construction paper in half and use the puncher to punch three holes along the folded edge. Then line up the pages evenly and tie some ribbon through each set of holes.
3. Help your child choose several pictures from the magazines that relate to his book topic. Cut out the pictures and paste them on the pages of the book.
4. Ask your child to tell you his story while you write the words under each picture.
5. Write the title of the book on the front cover and let your child write his name.
6. Read the book to your child and then let him tell it back to you.

COOKING:
CHILD-FRIENDLY WILDLY SPICED APPLE MUFFINS

The smell of cinnamon, ginger and apples often filled our home when our children were young…these muffins were a favorite with breakfast, lunch or dinner! *You will need: ¼ cup canola oil, 1 apple peeled, cored and chopped, ¼ cup honey, 2 eggs, 1/3 cup milk, 1¾ cups flour, 1 tsp baking powder, 2 tsp ground cinnamon, 1 tsp ground ginger, ½ cup unsweetened applesauce, ½ cup raisins, 1 greased 12-cup regular muffin tin, electric mixer, and a large bowl.*

1. Put the oil and honey in the bowl and beat with the mixer until creamy.
2. Add the eggs and mix until blended. Then add the milk and mix until smooth.
3. Mix in the flour a little at a time. Add the baking powder, cinnamon and ginger.
4. Add the chopped apple, raisins, and applesauce and stir until well blended.
5. Spoon the batter into the muffin cups and bake at 350 degrees for 30 minutes.
6. Makes 12 muffins. Cool and then store in an airtight container.

READING:
ALEXANDER AND THE TERRIBLE, HORRIBLE, NO GOOD, VERY BAD DAY

Written by Judith Viorst
Illustrated by Ray Cruz
(New York: Atheneum, 1972)

Alexander is having a terrible, horrible, no good, very bad day. He wakes up with gum in his hair, his favorite sweater falls into the sink and gets wet, his brothers get prizes in their cereal boxes while he only gets cereal in his, and at school, his best friend finds a new best friend. The day ends just as badly…he hates the lima beans that are part of dinner, his bath water is too hot and the cat no longer wants to sleep with him, preferring to cuddle up with one of Alexander's brothers. Although Alexander doesn't seem to get any sympathy from his mother, she does reassure him by telling him that everyone has days like this sometimes.

POSITIVE PARENTAL PARTICIPATION NOTE:

How many negative emotions did Alexander have to cope with on his no good, very bad day? Jealousy, anger, rejection, sadness…our young children have these feelings also. Listening to your child helps validate the feelings that he has…he can't always find the prize in his cereal box, and he needs to know that it is acceptable to be unhappy about it. You can also reassure him that no matter how bad things seem, you will always be there for him and that you love him, even when he is having a no good, very bad day.

NOTES:

_____

_____

_____

_____

_____

_____

_____

CRAFTING:
RHYTHM BAND DRUM

Children love drums...they love to beat out their own rhythm...it is also an excellent way to dissipate some negative emotions in a constructive manner.

You will need: 1 empty, cylindrical oatmeal box or coffee can with plastic lid, construction paper, paste, and crayons or markers.

1. Let your child draw some pictures or designs on a piece of construction paper.
2. Roll the paper around the box or can and paste it in place.
3. Use a spoon for the drumstick and let your child drum along to a music tape.

COOKING:
CHILD-FRIENDLY MINESTRONE SOUP

Poor Alexander...his no good, very bad day ended with lima beans for dinner...and he hated lima beans. Lima beans are in this delicious minestrone soup...your child may give them a try because he helped to prepare the soup.

You will need: 2 cups shredded cabbage, 2 Tb olive oil, 1 cup chopped onion, 1 28-ounce can whole tomatoes (you will also use the juice), 1 tsp honey, 1 tsp dried basil, 2 cups carrots peeled and chopped, 1 cup chopped celery, 5½ cups water, ¼ pound uncooked spaghetti broken in quarters, 1 10-ounce can red kidney beans rinsed and drained, 1 10-ounce box frozen lima beans, ¼ tsp salt, 6 Tb freshly-grated Parmesan cheese, and a large pot with a cover.

1. In a large pot, heat olive oil on medium-low and sauté onions about 4 minutes.
2. Stir in tomatoes, honey and basil, cabbage, carrots and celery and water.
3. Bring to a boil, uncovered, over high heat.
4. Add the beans, cover and simmer on low about 1 hour, stirring occasionally.
5. Add the spaghetti and cook 15 minutes. Garnish each serving with Parmesan cheese, if desired.
6. Makes 6-10 servings. Refrigerate or freeze leftovers in airtight containers.

READING:
SORRY

Written by Jean Van Leeuwen
Illustrated by Brad Sneed
(New York: Phyllis Fogelman Books, 2001)

Two brothers, Ebenezer and Obadiah, live together amicably in a small house in mountain country, sharing the farm chores by day and playing music on the front porch every evening. One morning, Obadiah criticizes the oatmeal that Ebenezer made for breakfast and Ebenezer dumps the bowl of oatmeal over Obadiah's head. The brothers refuse to speak to each other and go about their chores in silence for the rest of the day. In the days that follow, they avoid being in the same room with each other. Finally, Obadiah takes a saw, cuts the house in half and moves his half of the house across the field to the next hilltop. Although many years pass and their families grow with children and grandchildren, the brothers refuse to have anything to do with each other. One day, Ebenezer's great-grandson meets Obadiah's great-grandson at the wall that separates the properties and, although their relationship begins on a hostile note, they are able to reconcile their differences by talking to each other and saying, "I'm sorry."

POSITIVE PARENTAL PARTICIPATION NOTE:

Communication is definitely the key to living peacefully and happily with others (and with oneself). Although we sometimes say things that hurt someone else's feelings, we can apologize and talk about it and find an amicable solution. We need to help our children learn to talk about how they feel, honestly and openly. By accepting your child's negative feelings as well as his positive ones, you help empower him and build his self-esteem.

NOTES:

_____

_____

_____

CRAFTING:
PAPER ROLL FLUTE

Music is an important form of communication. As a parent, you can provide many musical experiences for your child by listening to varied types music, attending concerts and offering your child the opportunity to play different musical instruments.

You will need: 1 empty toilet paper roll, 1 rubber band, 1 piece of wax paper, a sharp pencil, and crayons or markers.

1. Use the point of the pencil to make 3 holes along the side of the toilet paper roll.
2. Cover one end of the roll with wax paper and hold in place with the rubber band.
3. Hum into the uncovered end while you move your fingers over the holes.
4. Your child can decorate the flute by coloring the outside with markers or crayons.

COOKING:
CHILD-FRIENDLY CORN CHOWDER

Milk from Obadiah's cows and corn from Ebenezer's cornfields...if only they had pooled their resources, they would have been able to enjoy this delicious soup!

You will need: 1 Tb margarine, 2 onions (peeled and chopped), 1 sweet green pepper (cored, seeded and chopped), 2 10-oz packages of frozen whole kernel corn, 3 cups milk, salt to taste, yogurt and/or parsley for garnish, and a large pot with a cover.

1. Heat margarine in the pot. Sauté the onions and green pepper for 10 minutes.
2. Add the corn, cover, and simmer on low for 10-12 minutes. Then add milk and simmer an additional 5 minutes. If desired, puree soup in blender before serving.
3. Ladle into the bowls...top with a spoonful of yogurt and/or a sprig of parsley, if desired. Makes 6 servings.

READING:
FLYAWAY KATIE

Written and illustrated by Polly Dunbar
(Cambridge, MA: Candlewick Press, 2004)

Katie is feeling "gray". She passes by a picture of exotic birds and she decides to use colorful clothing and paints to brighten up her sad mood. She does this and she is able to spend the day in a happy state of mind.

POSITIVE PARENTAL PARTICIPATION NOTE:

We all have "gray" days. Young children need to learn that they can influence, and to some extent control, the way they feel. Of course, as a parent, you probably don't want to encourage your child to paint her face blue and put orange stripes on her arms. You can, however, encourage your child to tell you how she is feeling. When your child trusts that you will not judge her or criticize her for her feelings, she will be more likely to share her confidences.

NOTES:

_____
_____
_____
_____
_____
_____
_____
_____
_____
_____
_____
_____

CRAFTING:
VIBRANT SPONGE PAINTING

Young children love to paint, make messes, and see their artwork hanging in a place of honor…you can help brighten your child's mood and boost her self-esteem with this project.

You will need: Paper plates (one for each color), a clean sponge cut into quarters, non-toxic tempera paints, construction or painting paper, and cover-ups for protecting clothes and the work surface.

1. Put on cover-ups to protect clothing and cover the work surface.
2. Pour a small amount of paint onto a plate. Do this for each color being used.
3. Press a small piece of sponge into the color and then press onto the paper.
4. When dry, hang the pictures to lift everyone's mood.

Important tip: Talk to your child about the colors she is creating as one color blends with another.

COOKING:
CHILD-FRIENDLY RAINBOW FRUIT AND
RICE PUDDING PARFAITS

Color does lift one's mood…help your child create a multi-colored dessert for the entire family to enjoy…when everyone compliments her for the delicious and beautiful treat, her self-esteem will be lifted also. *You will need: 1½ cups cooked brown rice, ¼ cup honey, ½ cup coconut flakes, 1 cup pineapple chunks, 1 sliced banana, ½ cup blueberries, ½ cup sliced strawberries, 1 cup yogurt, a large bowl, and 4 parfait glasses*

1. Mix the rice, honey, yogurt, and coconut in a large bowl.
2. Drop a spoonful of this mixture into each parfait glass.
3. Now spoon in some pineapple chunks and cover with another spoonful of the rice mixture.
4. Add a spoonful of sliced strawberries and cover with the remaining rice mixture.
5. Top with blueberries.

Important tip: You and your child can layer the fruit in whatever order you choose. In addition, you can use your imagination to substitute different fruits.

READING:
HOOT AND HOLLER

Written by Alan Brown
Illustrated by Rimantas Rolia
(New York: Alfred A. Knopf, 2001)

Holler, a big owl, and Hoot, a little owl, played together every night in the woods. They were both shy, and neither friend spoke of how he felt about the other. A storm separated the two owls and each worried that he would never find his best friend. A wise old owl advised Holler to call out loudly for Hoot. Although Holler was very shy, and had never been able to raise his voice, he found the courage to call very loudly and Hoot heard him. They found each other and were overjoyed and were finally able to express their feelings of love.

POSITIVE PARENTAL PARTICIPATION NOTE:

How difficult it is sometimes to express one's feelings! We can help our children by being good role models...don't wait for a special occasion to tell your child that you love him. Children need to know that they are loved every day of their lives. And, although the verbal confirmation of your love is important, you need to show your child as well...with Positive Parental Participation!

NOTES:

_____

_____

_____

_____

_____

_____

_____

CRAFTING:
MAKE AN OWL CRAYON/MARKER STORAGE BOX

You can help your child be more organized (which helps decrease frustration and stress) with this storage box for crayons and markers. He will always know where to find his writing materials and you won't be picking up his art supplies off the floor. *You will need: One shoebox or other sturdy box of similar size, construction paper in three colors, paste, and a pair of scissors.*

1. Cut a piece of paper a little longer and wider than the short side of the box. Paste it in place…this will be the body of the owl.

2. Cut two sets of three different size (and color) circles…1 inch, 2 inches and 3 inches across. Paste the small onto the medium and the medium onto the large. Do this for the other set of circles and paste in place…these are the owl's eyes.

3. Cut a small triangle and paste into place between the eyes…this is the nose.

4. Cut a circle about 3 inches across and then cut it in half and cut notches on the straight side and paste in place…these are the claws.

5. Cut a piece of construction paper in half and then fold it like an accordion and paste in place at the sides of the box…these are the wings.

COOKING:
SOFT-BAKED OWL-EYES PRETZELS

You will need: 1¼ cups warm water, 1 package active dry yeast, 1 Tb sugar, ½ tsp salt, 3¼ cups flour, 1 egg, 1 Tb water, 2 Tb coarse sea salt, 2 greased cookie sheets, a large bowl, a small bowl, wire racks, and a pastry brush. Preheat oven to 425 degrees.

1. Pour warm water into the large bowl, sprinkle the yeast and let stand 5 minutes. Stir with spoon until blended. Add sugar, ½ tsp salt and 1 cup of flour and blend.

2. Add 2 more cups of flour, ½ cup at a time, stirring until well blended.

3. Knead the dough on a floured surface until smooth and elastic.

4. Divide the dough into 12 pieces. Roll each piece into a rope about 15 inches long and coil it for owl eyes, then place on the baking sheets.

5. Break the egg into the small bowl and mix in 1 Tb of water. Brush egg mixture over each pretzel and then sprinkle with coarse salt. Bake 15 minutes till golden.

READING:
GOODBYE MOUSIE

Written by Robie Harris
Illustrated by Jan Ormerod
(NY: Margaret K. McElderry Books, 2001)

A little boy goes through several stages of grief when his pet mouse dies…first denial, then anger, then sadness. His mother and father listen to him, sympathize with his loss, and try to help him deal with his feelings. His mother gives him a shoebox and they put the dead mouse in it, along with several items that the little boy chooses. Then the boy paints the box and his parents help him bury his pet.

POSITIVE PARENTAL PARTICIPATION NOTE:

Often, the first death a child experiences is the loss of a beloved pet. Although at times, a parent may not think highly of a particular pet, it is important to acknowledge the feelings that your child is experiencing. With this acknowledgment, your child understands that he is of value and as he grows, he will be able to value others, as well.

NOTES:

_____

_____

_____

_____

_____

_____

_____

_____

_____

CRAFTING:
SOAP-BUBBLE FINGERPAINT

Being able to get your hands full of squishy stuff with your
mother's approval results in a very happy child!
*You will need: ¼ cup liquid laundry soap, 1 Tb corn starch, 1 tsp
dishwashing liquid, a mixing bowl or jar, finger paint paper (freezer paper is a good substitute), and
cover-ups for the "workers" and the work surface.*

1. Make sure you, your child, and the surface you are working on are well covered (finger-painting is MESSY…that's part of the charm).
2. Mix all of the ingredients until well blended.
3. Start with a tablespoonful of the mixture…let your child spread it around on the paper and then he can make designs in it.

Important tip: If you want to color your finger paint add a few drops of non-toxic tempera paint or food coloring to the mixture.

COOKING:
CHILD-FRIENDLY STRAWBERRY JAM

There is something very comforting about toast…serve it with
this homemade strawberry jam and your child will be beaming
with pride because he made it!
*You will need: 1 quart of strawberries (fresh or frozen), 1 cup of
sugar or honey, a potato masher (or other utensil to crush the berries), and a large kettle or pot.*

1. If fresh, wash the strawberries and remove the stems and bruised spots.
2. Put into a large bowl (or directly into the pot) and crush.
3. Add the sugar or honey, mix well, and heat on low, stirring until the sugar or honey is dissolved.
4. Raise the heat and boil rapidly, uncovered, stirring often until thick.
5. Remove from the heat and let stand 1-2 minutes.
6. Pour or spoon carefully into clean Tupperware containers or jelly jars.
7. Refrigerate to store. Makes about 3-4 cups.

    Important tip: You can substitute other types of berries or a mixed variety, if you wish.

READING:
AFTER CHARLOTTE'S MOM DIED

Written by Cornelia Spelman
Illustrated by Judith Friedman
(Morton Grove, IL: Albert Whitman & Co., 1996)

When five-year old Charlotte's mother dies in a car accident, the little girl has many feelings she is not comfortable expressing to her dad, even though she loves him very much. She worries about going to sleep because an aunt told her that dying was like going to sleep. She is angry and sad and scared, although on the outside she still looks the same. After an incident at school alerts her father to the fact that Charlotte is not dealing well with the death of her mother, he decides to go with Charlotte to see a therapist. The therapist helps them to talk about how they feel and they realize that although they will continue to feel sad about the death of Charlotte's mother, they can find happiness in life.

POSITIVE PARENTAL PARTICIPATION NOTE:

This author has written a number of books that deal with the sensitive subject of death. As important as her tender stories are to young children, equally important are the prefaces that give adults much-needed advice on how to approach this difficult issue with their children. The bottom line…listen carefully to your child, acknowledge his fears and feelings without judging, offer assurances that there will always be people to love him and care for him, and offer hope for future happiness.

NOTES:
_____
_____
_____
_____
_____
_____
_____

CRAFTING:
TREASURE BOX SHOEBOX

Memories of special people, places and experiences are extremely important for all of us. Help your child start a box of treasured mementos now!

You will need: A shoebox with a lid, paper to cover the box (gift wrap, shelf paper, painting paper), scissors, and paste.

1. Cut the paper your child has selected to cover the box. You will need two pieces, one for the box and one for the lid. Important tip: If you use painting paper, your child can decorate it with vegetable prints, sponge painting or pictures cut from magazines or old greeting cards.
2. Carefully fit the paper around the outside of the shoebox and paste in place. Do the same for the lid.
3. Make a label to put on the box, for example, EMILY'S TREASURED MEMENTOS or JOSH'S BOX OF MEMORIES.

COOKING:
CHILD-FRIENDLY BANANA-BANANA CREAM PIE

Simple Simon met a pie-man going to the fair. We have cakes and pies for special occasions and for entertaining company. Make this delicious pie (bananas and milk provide important nutrients) with your child...the special occasion...you are together!

You will need: 1 ready-to-use graham cracker crust, 1 package of instant banana pudding (3.9 oz), 1½ cups cold milk, 2 sliced bananas, a can of whipped cream, a bowl, and a whisk.

1. In the bowl, combine the banana pudding mix and the 1½ cups of milk.
2. Stir until well blended and slightly thick and pour into the cracker crust.
3. Chill in the refrigerator until firm (about an hour) and then lay sliced bananas over the surface and cover with whipped cream.

READING:
NANA UPSTAIRS, NANA DOWNSTAIRS

Written and illustrated by Tomie dePaola
(New York: G.P.Putnam's Sons, 1973)

Tommy enjoys visiting his grandmother, grandfather, and great-grandmother every Sunday. Even though his great-grandmother is very elderly and stays upstairs in her bedroom all the time, Tommy loves her very much and listens to her stories while they eat candy together. When Nana Upstairs dies, Tommy is very sad and he misses her. His parents comfort and reassure him that he will always have his memories of her.

POSITIVE PARENTAL PARTICIPATION NOTE:

Strong bonds are formed between individuals of different generations. We need to be honest with young children when older relatives are ill or dying and acknowledge their right to be sad, afraid or angry about the situation.

NOTES:
_____
_____
_____
_____
_____
_____
_____
_____
_____
_____
_____
_____

CRAFTING:
MAKE A FAMILY ALBUM

When our grown children come to visit, they love to look at
our many photo albums. Not only do they enjoy seeing
themselves at different ages and stages, they also love to look at
the pictures of their parents and grandparents when they were young. These old photos give
them a sense of belonging…a connection to something larger than themselves. By developing
this connection, your child's self-esteem grows. One way you can help him do this is to
construct a special family album that will belong to him.

*You will need: A selection of photos of the family (let your child choose the ones he wants from your
albums and then have copies made), a small photo album, paper cut to fit into the sleeves of the
album, and a fine line marker.*

1. Write your child's name and a title for the album (such as…MY WONDERFUL FAMILY)
on one of the pieces of paper and slip it into the first page of the album.
2. Let your child choose the photo for the next page and slip it into place. Have him tell you
something about that person (such as…My Grandpa has lots of hair on his face. He takes me
fishing.) Write that on a paper and slip it into the album sleeve opposite the photo. Continue
in this manner with the other photos your child has selected. Important tip: This is a lovely on-
going activity.

COOKING:
CHILD-FRIENDLY HOMEMADE FRUITY RAISIN
SORBET

*You will need: 2 cups chopped fruit (strawberries, blueberries, canned
peaches…use your imagination), 2 cups sliced banana, 1 cup orange
or pineapple, ½ cup raisins, blender and a large bowl.*

1. Freeze the fruit and the bananas until solid.
2. Put the frozen fruit in the blender with the juice and blend until stiff.
3. Scoop out of blender and stir in raisins.
4. Serve immediately or refreeze in a covered container.
5. Makes 6-8 servings, about 2 cups. Best eaten within a few days.

NOTES:

CHAPTER FIVE: "I'M AFRAID!"

How to help your child acknowledge and cope with his fears

Four-year old Michael warily eyes his mother as she enters his bedroom. "Time to get up, Michael," she says. "We have to be at the hospital by 10:00." Michael's eyes fill with tears and he begins to cry. "Don't wanna go to the hospital; wanna stay here." His mother sits down on the side of the bed and allows Michael to crawl onto her lap. She holds him in a warm and loving embrace, rocking him gently while she places soft kisses on the top of his bandaged head. "We need to go so the doctor can take the stitches out," she

> *"The only thing we have to fear is fear itself."*
> **Winston Churchill**

tells him. His mother continues, "But Nana sent a special book for you and it's all about George, the curious monkey and the time he had to go to the hospital." Michael's sobbing quiets as he reaches for the book his mother had set down on the bed. "Did George really have to go to the hospital?" asks Michael. "And did he have stitches in his head, too?" "Let's find out," says his mother, smiling as she begins to read ***Curious George Goes To The Hospital*** by H. A. Rey. When the story is finished, Michael giggles and says, "George was a silly monkey to eat a piece of puzzle. Puzzle pieces don't look like candy. Can I have a piece of candy now?" His mother laughs and replies, "After you get dressed, we have just enough time to make peanut butter balls and you can have one with breakfast. And, when we get back, we can make our own puzzle to take apart and put back together again." No longer frightened about his trip to the hospital, Michael gets dressed and, with his mother's help, measures out the peanut butter, honey and dried milk powder to make the candy-like treat. In the car, on the way to the hospital, Michael's mother begins to sing, "Ten Little Monkeys, Jumping on the Bed" and the four-year old joyfully joins in.

POSITIVE PARENTAL PARTICIPATION NOTE:

When your child is afraid of something, you can encourage him to voice that fear and then you need to listen without ridicule or condemnation. Even though the monster is not real, your child's fear is real and, by acknowledging that fear, you help your child step out on the road to coping with it. What are the fears of young children? Some of the most common are: fear of the dark and going to sleep, fear of monsters, fear of separation and getting lost, fear of new experiences and new places and fear of illness and death.

READING:
GILA MONSTERS MEET YOU AT THE AIRPORT

Written by Marjorie Weinman Sharmat
Illustrated by Byron Barton
(New York: Macmillan Publishing Company, 1980)

A little boy is moving out west with his family and is very apprehensive because he is sure that life there will be horrible. As his journey progresses, he realizes that there are some things that look very similar to his former home in New York City, and some things that look different. However, nothing looks scary (there were NO Gila monsters waiting to meet him at the airport even though his best friend had assured him that would happen) and he feels more confident and positive about his new home.

POSITIVE PARENTAL PARTICIPATION NOTE:

For children as well as for adults, the "unknown" is what we fear most. If your child has concerns about anything, you can help most by listening to him, and then by providing him with the knowledge he needs to put his fears to rest.

NOTES:

_____

_____

_____

_____

_____

_____

_____

_____

_____

_____

CRAFTING:
MAKE A TRANSPORTATION COLLAGE

You will need: Old magazines, construction paper, paste, and scissors (child-safe ones if your child will be doing the cutting).

1. Look through the magazines with your child and let him choose the pictures he wishes to have in his transportation collage (cars, trucks, buses, planes, etc.).
2. Cut out the pictures and let your child paste them onto the construction paper.
3. Cut strips from another piece of construction paper and glue around the edges.

Important tip: Hang up your child's artwork...he will know you are proud of his efforts.

COOKING:
CHILD-FRIENDLY VEGETARIAN CHILI

In the story, the little boy worries that he will have to eat chili and beans for breakfast, lunch and dinner. Many children have food fears and phobias. As a child, I dreaded going to visit my great-aunts because they always served meals that were unfamiliar to me. If your child is encouraged to help in meal preparation, he will be more likely to try new things, and each time he tries something new, he will gain more confidence to meet other challenges in life. *You will need: 2 Tbs. olive oil, 1 cup chopped onion, 2 Tb minced garlic, 2 cups diced tomatoes (canned or fresh), 1 cup canned red kidney beans and 1 cup pinto beans (rinsed and drained), ½ cup diced carrot, 2 tsp chili powder (optional), 1 Tb honey, ½ cup grated cheddar cheese, ½ cup yogurt, and a large pan with cover.*

1. Heat the oil in a pot over medium heat. Add onions, cook a few minutes while stirring, and then add garlic.
2. Add tomatoes, beans, carrot, chili powder (if desired) and honey. Bring to a boil, reduce heat, cover, and simmer for 45 minutes, stirring occasionally.
3. Garnish each serving with grated cheese and a dollop of yogurt. Serves 6-8.
4. Important tip: You may want to do some of the prep beforehand, such as chopping the onions and mincing the garlic...we want our young cooks smiling, not crying. In addition, your child can help measure the ingredients into a bowl and you can add them to the pan...we don't want young ones near hot pans and stovetops.

READING:
THERE'S AN ALLIGATOR UNDER MY BED

Written and illustrated by Mercer Mayer
(New York: Dial Books for Young Readers, 1987)

Although his parents are not able to see the alligator that lives under his bed, the little boy knows there is one there. He decides to lure the alligator into the garage so he will not have to deal with it anymore. One night, he scatters food (peanut butter sandwiches, pie, candy, cookies and an assortment of fruits and vegetables) from the garage, up the stairs, and all the way into his bedroom. When the alligator comes out from under the bed and starts to eat the food, the little boy hides and then stealthily follows the alligator as he makes his way towards the garage door, consuming all the food in his path. As soon as the alligator enters the garage, the boy slams the door, locks it, and then goes to sleep… proud that he has vanquished his foe.

POSITIVE PARENTAL PARTICIPATION NOTE:

Children love to hear about other children who rise to the challenges in their lives and succeed. By listening to your child and respecting him and his concerns, you are helping him gain the confidence he needs to face the challenges in his life and seek new ones.

NOTES:

_____
_____
_____
_____
_____
_____
_____
_____
_____
_____

CRAFTING:
EGG CARTON ALLIGATORS

You will need: Corrugated egg carton, green paint or marker, construction paper in black, white, green and red, paste, and scissors.

1. Cut the bottom portion of the egg carton in half. Turn one strip upside down and paint the sections green and let dry.
2. Cut 2 (one-inch) circles of white and 2 (1/2-inch) circles of black. Paste the black circle on the white circle and attach to one side of the first section for the eye. Do the same on the other side for the other eye.
3. Cut a two-inch oval from red paper and attach underneath the first section for the tongue.
4. Cut 4 two-inch ovals from green paper and attach underneath on each side of the second and fourth section for the legs and feet.
5. Important tip: The alligator in the story did not have a name...perhaps your child can think of a good one.

COOKING:
CHILD-FRIENDLY VEGETABLE SALAD

Many children refuse to eat vegetables...perhaps they observe the expression on adults' faces and take their cue from that. Children are more likely to eat something they have helped prepare. The edible bowl and bright colors make this great to look at and fun to eat. If you want to feed more than two people, increase the ingredients.

You will need: 2 pre-formed salad bowl tacos, 2 cups shredded lettuce, ½ cup steamed carrots sliced thin, ½ cup tomatoes diced, ½ cup cucumber diced, ½ cup steamed broccoli florets, ½ cup steamed cauliflower florets, 2 Tb olive oil, 2 Tb grated Parmesan cheese, and a microwave-safe bowl.

1. Wash all of the vegetables and put carrots, broccoli, cauliflower and 1 Tb of water in a bowl, cover with waxed paper and microwave on high for one minute.
2. Mix lettuce and vegetables in mixing bowl and toss with olive oil. Spoon the mixture into the taco bowls and sprinkle with grated Parmesan cheese.

READING:
ANGUS LOST

Written and illustrated by Marjorie Flack
(New York: Doubleday, 1932)

Angus, a little terrier, is bored with his home and yard and decides to see what the world is like. After several scary adventures, Angus wants very much to go home, but he cannot find his way. He spends the night hiding in a cave, trembling in fear the entire time. In the morning, he hears the familiar sound of the milkman's horse and wagon and eagerly follows them from house to house as the milkman makes his deliveries. Finally, Angus recognizes his very own yard and is relieved to be home at last.

POSITIVE PARENTAL PARTICIPATION NOTE:

Many young children worry about getting lost or separated from those they love and, although we want to encourage curiosity and independence in our children, we are responsible for keeping them safe from harm. Teaching your child his name, address and phone number and what to do in case he is ever lost is very important and will enable him to feel more confident about his own ability to deal with such a situation. Reassure your child that you will always find him, no matter what...this will contribute to his feeling of safety. That feeling of safety and his confidence in his own ability to deal with difficult situations will encourage him to overcome his fears and try new experiences.

NOTES:

_____

_____

_____

_____

_____

_____

_____

CRAFTING:
NATURE PICTURE

You will need: Paper, assorted leaves and twigs, and glue.

1. Take a walk to a nearby park, pointing out landmarks that you pass. In the park, let your child choose a selection of leaves and twigs. See if your child remembers any of the landmarks on the way back.
2. Let your child glue the various nature items he collected onto the construction paper. Hang the picture in your home…what a boost to your child's self-esteem.

Important tip: Make sure you check each item that your child wants to pick up…some things are better left where they are!

COOKING:
CHILD-FRIENDLY HOMEMADE BUTTER

Although it happened over fifty years ago, I still remember licking the cream off the cardboard caps that sealed the bottles of milk that the milkman had delivered to my grandmother's house. These days, most of us buy all of our groceries at the store, including milk and butter. Take this opportunity to make some butter at home! *You will need: 1 cup of heavy whipping cream, electric mixer, and a large bowl.*

1. Pour the cream into the bowl and beat on medium till stiff peaks are formed (about 1-2 minutes)…this is REAL WHIPPED CREAM! Taste some for an out-of-this-world treat!
2. Continue beating (about 4-8 minutes) and soon the curds will separate from the whey. (You could sing "Little Miss Muffet" with your child while you are doing this and do the finger play later)
3. Pour off the whey and you will be left with a lump of pure butter.
4. Enjoy with crackers, bread or toast.
5. Put in a covered container and store in the refrigerator.

Important tip: Instead of using an electric mixer, you could put the cream in a glass jar with a lid and shake…but this will take between 5-30 minutes and little hands might get tired.

READING:
BLUEBERRIES FOR SAL

Written and illustrated by Robert McCloskey
(New York: Viking Press, 1948)

One summer day, a little girl named Sal goes with her mother to pick blueberries on Blueberry Hill. Since she eats the blueberries almost as quickly as her mother picks them, her mother tells Sal to pick some of her own. Meanwhile, a bear cub is also on a blueberry hunt with his mother. Both Sal and Little Bear become separated from their own mothers and inadvertently begin following the wrong mother. Fortunately, the mix-up is resolved and both Sal and Little Bear are reunited with the correct parent.

POSITIVE PARENTAL PARTICIPATION NOTE:

Very young children often get anxious when they lose sight of their parents because they are afraid their parents will not return. This story reassures young children that even if that happens (or their parents leave them at day care when they go to work or with a sitter when they go out to shop), the separation will only be a temporary one.

NOTES:

_____

_____

_____

_____

_____

_____

_____

_____

_____

_____

_____

CRAFTING:
PAINTING WITH BLUEBERRY INK

It is important for children to learn how things were done long ago, before shopping malls and stores offered every imaginable item twenty-four hours a day. Self-sufficiency is one of the building blocks of self-esteem.

You will need: 1 cup blueberries, bowl, potato masher or other utensil to squash the berries, construction or painting paper, toothpicks, Q-Tips, plastic gloves and cover-ups.

1. Squash blueberries in a bowl and strain the juice.
2. Dip a toothpick and/or Q-Tip in the berry "ink" and use it to draw on the paper. Important tip: Blueberry ink can stain…cover hands, clothing and work surfaces.

COOKING:
CHILD-FRIENDLY BLUEBERRY MUFFINS

I can still hear the "plink, plink" as the first blueberries my children picked made their way into the containers. At the time, we lived in an old farmhouse in a small Connecticut town and the backyard was a paradise of fruit trees and, best of all, over 100 blueberry bushes. Here is the blueberry muffin recipe we used.

You will need: 1 cup fresh blueberries, ½ cup sugar, 1½ cups flour, ½ tsp baking soda, ¼ cup canola oil, 2 eggs beaten, ½ cup milk, two bowls and 1 greased 12-muffin pan.

1. Preheat oven to 375 degrees. Lightly grease muffin pan. Rinse off blueberries.
2. In a large bowl, combine sugar, flour, and baking soda.
3. In a small bowl, combine oil, milk, and beaten eggs.
4. Add liquid ingredients into dry ingredients and stir till just blended.
5. Fold blueberries into the batter and pour batter into prepared pan, until each cup is about 2/3 full.
6. Bake 18-20 minutes or until muffins are lightly browned and cooked through. Insert a toothpick into the center of a muffin…muffins are done if it comes out clean. The muffins retain their heat for quite awhile…let them cool and cut in half before serving to your child.

READING:
HARRY AND THE TERRIBLE WHATZIT

Written and illustrated by Dick Gackenbach
(New York: Clarion Books, 1977)

Harry is facing a dilemma. He has always avoided going down in the cellar because it is dark and damp and smells bad and he is sure there are monsters. However, when his mother goes down there to get a jar of pickles and doesn't return right away, Harry must make a decision. He goes down to the cellar to rescue his mother, armed with a broom. He confronts the giant double-headed monster that has been hiding behind the furnace and the monster gets smaller and smaller and finally leaves.

POSITIVE PARENTAL PARTICIPATION NOTE:

Everyone faces monsters of one sort or another. You can help your child master his monster by listening to his concerns and treating both your child and his concerns with respect. Never laugh at or make light of your child's fears…they are real, even if the monster is not. Not only will you gain his trust and confidence by listening with compassion, but you will also help his self-esteem to grow.

NOTES:

_____

_____

_____

_____

_____

_____

_____

_____

_____

_____

CRAFTING:
MAKE A SILLY MONSTER SOCK PUPPET

You will need: Clean sock (big enough to fit comfortably over your child's hand), magic markers, buttons or pieces of felt (for eyes and nose), yarn (for hair), ribbons and glue or thread and needle.

1. Attach the buttons or felt circles for eyes and nose (you can sew or glue them) or use markers to draw the features.
2. Attach the yarn for hair and tie several ribbons to the hair...the sillier the monster looks, the better.

Important tip: Put on a puppet show with your child while you reread the story. Your child can be Harry and vanquish his sock puppet monster.

COOKING:
CHILD-FRIENDLY HOMEMADE PICKLES

When my children were small and we lived in an old Connecticut farmhouse, our cellar was much like Harry's...dark and damp and sometimes it even smelled bad. The saving grace was an area of shelves filled with jars of fruits and vegetables I had preserved from our garden's harvest...spiced Seckel pears, cinnamon applesauce, and, of course, crisp, green pickles. Here is an easy recipe for that tasty condiment!

You will need: ½ cup onion, 1 cup cucumber, ½ cup vinegar, 4 Tbs. water, 4 Tbs. sugar, ¼ tsp salt, 1 Tb chopped parsley, and a 1 quart glass jar or bowl with cover.

1. Cut onion and cucumber into thin slices.
2. Put slices into 1-quart glass jar or bowl and mix with chopped parsley.
3. In a separate bowl, mix the vinegar, water, sugar, and salt.
4. Pour this liquid into the jar with the onion and cucumber.
5. Cover and refrigerate 24 hours before eating.
6. Keep the unused portion in the refrigerator.

READING:
DON'T WORRY, I'LL FIND YOU

Written and illustrated by Anna Grossnickle Hines
(New York: E.P. Dutton, 1986)

Sarah and her mother go to the mall to buy Sarah some new clothes. The little girl insists on taking her doll, Abigail. After a long and tiring morning of visiting many stores and trying on lots of clothes, Sarah puts Abigail on a chair while she tries on shoes and forgets to take her doll when she and her mother leave the store. Passing a toy store, Sarah remembers that she has left her doll behind and she hurries back to the shoe store without telling her mother. Although she finds Abigail right away, she soon realizes that she has lost her mother. Remembering her mother's instructions to "stay put", Sarah goes back to the toy store and waits there. Meanwhile, Sarah's mother has been checking all the stores and soon mother and child are reunited.

POSITIVE PARENTAL PARTICIPATION NOTE:

I'm sure Sarah's mother was tempted to scold her daughter, not only for walking away on her own, but also for bringing the doll, even though she had been advised to leave it at home. Fortunately, she chose to commend her daughter for obeying her instructions to stay where she was in case she got lost. In the future, Sarah will be more likely to follow other rules she is given and, even though she was frightened, her self-esteem was enhanced because she was able to keep some amount of control in the situation by following her mother's instructions.

NOTES:

_____

_____

_____

_____

_____

_____

CRAFTING:
POTATO PRINT PAINTINGS

You will need: 1 uncooked potato, fork, paper, 2 colors of tempera paints, 1 sponge cut in half, and 2 clean plastic containers (such as from margarine or cottage cheese).

1. Cut the potato in half and let your child use a fork to make a design.
2. Put a piece of sponge in each container and pour some paint on it.
3. Press the cut side of the potato onto the sponge and then onto the paper.

Important tip: You can use other fruits and veggies for printing.

COOKING:
CHILD-FRIENDLY OVEN-BAKED FRENCH FRIES

One potato, two potato, three potato four…five potato, six potato, seven potato, more! Not only are potatoes an inexpensive and versatile vegetable, they are also good for you, and, best of all, children love them! In the story, Sarah had french fries with her meal. Here is a healthy alternative to deep fat frying…and it tastes good, too!

You will need: 2 potatoes (Russet, Idaho or Yukon Gold all work well in this recipe), 1 Tb olive oil, pinch of salt, basil and oregano, and a lightly greased baking pan.

1. Preheat oven to 400 degrees and wash potatoes, cutting them in quarters.
2. Dry the potato pieces with a paper towel and put them in a bowl with the salt, basil, oregano and olive oil and toss so the pieces are coated.
3. Lay the pieces on one cut side on lightly greased baking pan and bake 10 minutes.
4. Carefully remove the pan and flip each potato onto the other cut side.
5. Bake an additional 10-15 minutes till the potatoes are golden brown outside.

This recipe makes enough for two adults or three children, depending on appetites. Just increase the ingredients to feed more people.

READING:
CURIOUS GEORGE GOES TO THE HOSPITAL

Written and illustrated by Margret & H.A. Rey
(Boston: Houghton Mifflin Company, 1966)

George, the curious little monkey, discovers a box on his friend's desk and cannot resist the temptation to open it. Of course, George does not know that the box contains a puzzle and, seeing all the colorful pieces, he wonders if it is candy and he swallows one puzzle piece. Later that day, his friend puts the puzzle together and discovers one piece is missing. George is afraid to tell his friend that he ate it and, the next morning, George wakes up feeling very ill. When his friend takes him to the hospital, an X-ray reveals the piece of puzzle stuck in his stomach. George has to stay in the hospital for a few days so that the doctors can remove the puzzle piece.

POSITIVE PARENTAL PARTICIPATION NOTE:

We need to try to be non-judgmental with our young children because, if they fear being laughed at, yelled at, or ignored by us, they will soon refrain from confiding in us. Developing a relationship of trust and communication with your child is critically important if you want him to gain a positive self-image. In addition, young children need to be reassured that doctors, dentists and hospitals are there to help them feel better and stay healthy.

NOTES:

_____

_____

_____

_____

_____

_____

_____

_____

_____

_____

CRAFTING:
MAKING YOUR OWN PUZZLE

Young children learn while they play...and most love playing with puzzles. They develop confidence each time they are able to fit the pieces together...and look for bigger challenges with each success.

You will need: An old magazine, 1 piece of heavy construction paper, 1 piece of cardboard the same size to use as the base, paste, and scissors.

1. Let your child choose a picture from an old magazine.
2. Paste the picture on the piece of construction paper.
3. When dry, cut the mounted picture into pieces. Depending on the age of your child, it can be a two or three or four or more piece puzzle.
4. Let your child put the pieces together to form the picture again.

COOKING:
CHILD-FRIENDLY NO-COOK FUDGE

George thought the puzzle pieces were candy...you can help your child make homemade fudge...to eat a bit and perhaps give some away as gifts.

You will need: One 12-oz package of chocolate chips, one 14-oz can sweetened condensed milk, microwave-safe bowl, 8-inch square well-greased pan, optional: 64 foil or paper muffin cups, optional: toppings of your choice (nuts or mini-marshmallows).

1. Mix chips and milk in the bowl, heat in microwave for 1 minute on high.
2. Stir and heat another minute, then stir. Heat for 30 seconds if not smooth.
3. Pour the mixture into the greased pan and let cool a few minutes.
4. Score with a knife into one-inch squares and press topping gently, but firmly onto each square. When cool (several hours), cut along scored lines and, using a spatula, put squares in individual muffin cups and store in covered container.

READING:

ALEXANDER, WHO'S NOT (DO YOU HEAR ME? I MEAN IT!) GOING TO MOVE

Written by Judith Viorst
Illustrated by Robin Glasser
(New York: Atheneum Books for Young Readers, 1995)

Alexander is very anxious about moving away from the friends and places he has grown accustomed to. He refuses to pack and talks to his father about the many alternative courses of action he could take to avoid moving. Fortunately, his parents let him know that they understand how difficult it is to leave familiar places and people behind. Alexander begins to think more positively about moving when his father offers to get a dog so that he will have an immediate friend at the new house.

POSITIVE PARENTAL PARTICIPATION NOTE:

Children feel comfortable and secure in the surroundings they are familiar with and often get worried and anxious if they have to move to a new home or even meet an unfamiliar person or have a new experience. Listening to your child helps him know that you value him and his ideas and that, in turn, helps give him the courage and confidence to face his fears and anxieties and overcome them.

NOTES:

_____

_____

_____

_____

_____

_____

_____

_____

_____

CRAFTING:
BUILDING A GRAHAM CRACKER GINGERBREAD HOUSE

You will need: 1 batch Royal Icing (you can prepare this in advance: beat 3 egg whites and ¼ tsp cream of tartar till foamy. Gradually beat in 1 lb confectioners' sugar and then beat on high speed till very thick and glossy. Keep icing covered as you work), 1 box graham crackers, 1 clean pint or quart cardboard milk or juice container, assortment of small colorful candies, piece of cardboard, and tubes of gel icing.

1. Spread some icing on bottom of container and press onto cardboard. Hold in place 1 minute (the icing is the "glue" in this project).
2. Take one square of cracker and spread icing thinly on flat side and press gently but firmly onto container. Cover the entire container with crackers.
3. Add candies as decorations using the icing to stick them to the crackers…you can put icing on the "roof" as snow and use the gel icing to outline the door and windows. If the container shows in any places, just spread some royal icing and press candies there.
4. When your child is finished, you can spread some icing on the cardboard base (it will look like snow) and press in small cookies shaped like trees or gingerbread men. If you add food coloring to some of the royal icing, the "snow" can be green grass or a blue roof or whatever your child wishes…let his imagination soar!
5. Get your camera and take lots of pictures of your child with his beautiful Graham Cracker Gingerbread House!

COOKING:
CHILD-FRIENDLY LEMONADE

Like Alexander, many children try their hand at earning money by selling lemonade. My children did also…this is the recipe I used for my young entrepreneurs. *You will need: 4-6 lemons, 1 cup water, 4 Tb sugar, 4 cups water, and a pan.*

1. Heat sugar and 1 cup water in small saucepan till sugar is dissolved completely.
2. Extract juice from lemons, enough for 1 cup of juice.
3. Remove pan from heat and add the juice and 4 cups cold water.
4. Pour into a pitcher and refrigerate 30-40 minutes. Serves 6.

READING:
THROUGH MOON AND STARS AND NIGHT SKIES

Written by Ann Turner
Illustrated by James Graham Hale
(New York: A Charlotte Zolotow Book, 1990)

A couple from the United States adopts a young boy from a foreign land. He travels by plane to meet them for the first time and he is beset with many different fears...of flying and of all the new experiences he is having It takes time for him to become more comfortable in his new surroundings, but, with the loving reassurance of his new parents, the little boy adjusts to his new situation.

POSITIVE PARENTAL PARTICIPATION NOTE:

Fear of new experiences is one of the most common fears of all...not only young children are prey to it. How can you help your child overcome this sometimes-debilitating fear? You need to recognize what is going on and then you need to reassure the child that everything will be all right and that you love him, no matter what. Perhaps you can accompany your child to the new place (nursery school, dentist's office, etc.) before the actual appointment so that your child will feel more comfortable when he has to go there. Taking a camera along to take some pictures and then developing them and displaying them at home might also help demystify this strange and new place.

NOTES:

_____
_____
_____
_____
_____
_____

CRAFTING:
PHOTO DISPLAY BOARD

In the story, the adoptive parents send the little boy photos of themselves, their dog and their home, in hopes that he will feel more comfortable when he finally arrives. You can help your child make a display board for photos taken of new and strange places (or people). Perhaps your child can even take some of the pictures himself...this might help increase his comfort level and confidence. *You will need: Camera, large sheet of poster board (or store-bought cork bulletin board, construction paper, markers, and tacks or tape.*

1. Take pictures while on vacation, a walk or a visit to a new place. After they are printed, let your child choose a few he wants to mount on the display board.
2. Tape each picture to a piece of construction paper and write your child's description of the picture. Pin (or tape) the construction papers to the board...change pictures every week.

COOKING:
CHILD-FRIENDLY GAZPACHO SOUP

You will need: 4 cups diced ripe tomatoes (or salt-free canned), 1½ cup diced cucumber, ½ cup diced scallions, ½ cup each diced green and red bell pepper, ½ cup chopped red onion, 2 Tb olive oil, 1 Tb honey, ¼ cup sour cream or yogurt, and a blender or food processor.

1. Place all veggies in blender or food processor and blend for 2 or 3 minutes. If you like a chunkier version of this soup, reserve ½ to 1 cup of the veggie mixture and add after the honey and oil are blended in.
2. Add honey and oil and blend until smooth.
3. Chill at least 45 minutes. Garnish each portion with 1 Tb of sour cream or yogurt.
4. Makes about 5 cups. Store unused portions in airtight container in fridge.

READING:
TAKE A KISS TO SCHOOL

Written by Angela McAllister
Illustrated by Sue Hellard
(New York: Bloomsbury Children's Books, 2006)

Although Digby, a little otter, has fun during his first day at school, he is reluctant to go again. He tells his mother that there are so many things to remember (where to hang his coat, how to line up, etc.) and he is afraid he will forget some of them and be embarrassed. Digby's mother solves the problem by filling her hands with kisses and putting the kisses in her son's jacket pocket. During the day, whenever Digby feels uncomfortable or scared, he takes out one of the kisses and presses it to his cheek. Helping another classmate who is even more hesitant than he is enables Digby to forget his own fears and Digby finds that he is looking forward to the next school day.

POSITIVE PARENTAL PARTICIPATION NOTE:

Many of us are anxious about having new experiences, going to new places, or meeting new people. Digby's mother's pocketful of kisses kept her love for her son close to his heart, even though she could not be with him and, when Digby became involved in the activities and people at school, he no longer thought about how much he missed his mother. Perhaps if your child is hesitant to be left at nursery or day care, you can employ Digby's mother's idea. Once your child is involved in the activities, he will feel much more comfortable even if you are not there. Coping with and overcoming separation anxiety is a big step in your child's emotional development and you need to be sensitive and non-judgmental about his fears.

NOTES:

_____

_____

_____

_____

_____

CRAFTING:
FOOD CHART

This is a great lesson in classification…and lots of fun as well!

You will need: Poster board or construction paper, old magazines, scissors, glue, and a marker.

1. Talk about what various animals eat. You can look at the school lunchroom picture in the book. Cut out pictures of animals, people and food from magazines.
2. Draw several lines on the paper and glue each animal or person on one line and the corresponding food they eat on the same line.
3. Let your child choose a title for the chart.

COOKING:
PITA POCKET CHICKEN SANDWICH

Digby kept his mother's kisses in his pocket…you and your child can make a special sandwich using "pocket" pita bread.

You will need: For each sandwich: 1 pita bread, 1 small baked chicken cutlet, 2 slices of tomato, 1 Tb sprouts, 1 Tb mashed avocado, and 1 leaf Romaine lettuce.

1. Slice the pita so you can stuff the "pocket".
2. Spread avocado inside the pocket.
3. Insert the chicken, tomato, sprouts and lettuce.

Important tip: You can heat the pita bread before stuffing, in oven or toaster, if desired.

READING:
BILLY AND THE BIG NEW SCHOOL

Written by Laurence Anholt

Illustrated by Catherine Anholt

(Morton Grove, IL: Albert Whitman & Company, 1997)

Billy is worried about his upcoming first day of school. While feeding some birds outside his home, he notices a very small bird being picked on by the bigger birds. Billy's mother helps him take the bird inside to care for it and, by the next morning, the bird is better and Billy sets it free. During a class discussion about pets, Billy tells everyone about his recent experience with the little bird. When the teacher and his classmates clap, Billy's feelings of confidence and self-worth skyrocket.

POSITIVE PARENTAL PARTICIPATION NOTE:

The unknown is a fearful place, for adults and children alike. Before your child attends his first day of school (or nursery school or day care), plan an informal visit so he can meet the teacher, see the place, and have a chance to use some of the facilities. Knowledge is power, and we want to help our children feel they have a measure of control in their lives.

NOTES:

_____

_____

_____

_____

_____

_____

_____

_____

_____

_____

CRAFTING:
MAKING A BIRD FEEDER

You will need: 2 slices stale bread (broken in small pieces), ½ cup vegetable oil, ¼ cup chopped carrot or apple, ¼ cup nuts, ½ cup wild birdseed, and a 12 inch string.

1. Mix bread, oil, carrot or apple, and nuts.
2. Form ball with mixture and push string into center.
3. Roll in birdseed. When hardened, hang it on a branch and watch the birds feed!

COOKING:
CHILD-FRIENDLY BREAKFAST GRANOLA

The tantalizing aroma of cinnamon filled the kitchen as the children in my day care group waited for the homemade granola to cool. Each child had taken part in the preparation, from measuring out the ingredients and discussing how cinnamon smelled, to mixing everything in the big bowl. Here is that recipe…pour in a bowl, add milk and some sliced banana and enjoy!

You will need: 2 cups old-fashioned oatmeal, ½ cup shredded coconut, ½ cup hulled sunflower seeds, ½ cup wheat germ, ¼ cup honey, ¼ cup vegetable oil, ½ cup raisins, ½ tsp cinnamon, and a 3 qt microwave-safe bowl.

1. Mix all ingredients except for the raisins in a three-quart, heatproof glass bowl.
2. Microwave for three minutes, one minute at a time, stirring each time.
3. Stir again and microwave for an additional two minutes, one minute at a time.
4. Stir in the raisins and microwave for 30 seconds.

Makes about 4-5 cups of granola. Cool and then store in tightly covered container. Serve as cereal, as a snack or to top fruit or ice cream.

READING:
FRIZZY THE FEARFUL

Written by Marjorie Weinman Sharmat
Illustrated by John Wollner
(New York: Holiday House, 1983)

Poor little Frizzy Tiger! He is afraid of almost everything…high places and low places, the dark, loud noises, and pits in pit-less fruit. He avoids going places with his friends and misses out on many fun-filled activities because he doesn't want anyone to know how frightened he is. When he climbs a tree to help a friend even though he is terrified, Frizzy realizes that everyone has fears, and he begins to feel a little better about his own situation.

POSITIVE PARENTAL PARTICIPATION NOTE:

When your child voices his fears and concerns, he needs you to listen with empathy and respect. This will show him that he is loved and valued. Let him know that everyone is afraid of different things at different times in their lives…perhaps you can share an experience from your own childhood.

NOTES:

_____
_____
_____
_____
_____
_____
_____
_____
_____
_____
_____

CRAFTING:
MAKE A BADGE OF COURAGE

Perhaps your child has just been to the dentist for a cleaning and went without making a fuss. Maybe he has finished his first week of nursery school and, even though he was anxious about being separated from you, he managed to enjoy his time there. Here is a badge of courage you can pin on your child that affirms his willingness to overcome his fears and accept life's challenges. *You will need: 2 pieces of construction paper (1 light, 1 dark), aluminum foil, ribbon, paste, and scissors.*

1. Cut a 3-inch circle from dark paper and a 2-inch circle from aluminum foil and help your child paste the aluminum foil circle on the dark circle.
2. Cut a 1-inch circle from the light paper, write your child's name on it and help him paste it in the middle of the aluminum foil circle.
3. Paste the ribbon at the back of the badge so it hangs down a few inches.
4. Pin the badge to your child's shirt with a small safety pin.

COOKING:
CHILD-FRIENDLY "PIT-LESS" FRUIT SALAD

You will need: 1 banana, a small bunch of seedless grapes, 1 apple, 1 pear, 1 navel orange, and a few leaves of lettuce to use as the base.

1. Wash all the fruit and lettuce and put the lettuce leaves in the bowls.
2. Slice the apple and pear and arrange on the lettuce.
3. Peel the orange, separate into sections and arrange on the plate.
4. Peel the banana, slice and add to the arrangement.
5. Cut each grape in half and add to the salad.
6. Serves 2-3 as a main dish (add some grilled chicken strips or cheese cubes for protein) or 4-6 for a side salad or snack.

Important tip: If you cut one section of the orange and squeeze it over the fruit, it will keep the fruit from turning brown and everything will have a lovely orange flavor. If you wish, you can drizzle a little honey over the salad for a little sweetness.

READING:
GOODNIGHT MOON

Written by Margaret Wise Brown
Illustrated by Clement Hurd
(New York: Harper & Row Publishers, 1947)

This classic bedtime story has been helping little ones face the night for over sixty years. Little Bunny says goodnight to all the objects in his room and finally falls asleep. Mother (or Grandmother) Bunny sits knitting in the rocking chair until it gets too dark to see. She leaves when Little Bunny falls asleep.

Positive Parental Participation Note:

Children love routines, just like Little Bunny did. Having a bedtime routine helps your child wind down from the stimulation of the day and makes going to sleep just another step in the process. Each family will have different rituals (such as a prayer before going to sleep), traditions (such as a story before the light is turned off), or routines (such as washing hands and face, brushing teeth and then getting into pajamas).

NOTES:
_____
_____
_____
_____
_____
_____
_____
_____
_____
_____
_____
_____
_____

CRAFTING:
FRAME A PICTURE FOR YOUR CHILD'S ROOM

You will need: Old magazines, construction paper, paste, and scissors.

1. Let your child choose a picture he likes from an old magazine.
2. Cut it out and have him paste it onto the construction paper.
3. Cut 4 strips from another piece of construction paper and paste along the edges of the picture to form a frame.
4. Your child can draw designs on the frame. Hang it in his room.

COOKING:
CHILD-FRIENDLY MUESLI

Little Bunny had a "bowlful of mush" (the German word Musli comes from Mus meaning mush or puree) that was probably a light snack of cereal before going to bed. You and your child can make your own Muesli (with no preservatives or additives)…moistened with milk or juice, hot or cold, for breakfast or a light evening snack…it is delicious!

You will need: 2 cups quick rolled oats, 1 cup wheat flakes, 1 cup rye flakes, 2 Tb brown sugar, ½ cup hulled sunflower seeds, ½ cup wheat bran (optional), 1 cup raisins, ½ cup chopped dried fruit, ½ cup chopped raw nuts, a large bowl and a big glass jar with a lid.

1. Mix oats and flakes in bowl and add brown sugar, sunflower seeds and bran.
2. Add raisins, dried fruit and nuts, mix well and pour into jar.
3. Use as cereal with milk or juice, hot or cold (let the cereal absorb the liquid a little before eating), or as topping for ice cream, yogurt or fresh or canned fruit.
4. Makes about 6 cups of muesli.

Important tip: You can substitute a box of high-quality multi-grain cereal from the store if you can't get the wheat flakes, rye flakes and wheat bran.

READING:
FRANKLIN IN THE DARK

Written by Paulette Bourgeois
Illustrated by Brenda Clark
(New York: Scholastic Inc., 1987)

Franklin, the turtle, has a problem. He has to sleep in his shell, but he is afraid that there are monsters and other creepy things living inside of it. His mother tries to reassure him by shining a flashlight into the shell, but Franklin is still concerned. He talks to some of the other animals and discovers that each one is afraid of something, but all have found some way to cope with their fears. Franklin tells his mother about his day and goes to sleep in his shell, even though he is still afraid…but he is comforted by the night light he turns on.

POSITIVE PARENTAL PARTICIPATION NOTE:

How can you help your child with his fears? First of all, by acknowledging what they are…your child needs to trust that you will not judge him or love him less if he is to confide in you. Secondly, you and your child can examine the situation and try to find a way for him to alleviate that fear.

NOTES:

_____
_____
_____
_____
_____
_____
_____
_____
_____
_____
_____

CRAFTING:
PAPER PLATE TURTLES

You will need: 1 paper plate, green paint, black marker, green and black construction paper, paste, and scissors.

1. Paint or color the underside of the plate green and let dry. Then draw designs on the green with the marker for the markings of the turtle's shell.
2. Cut out 4 legs, 1 head and 1 tail from the green construction paper and paste in place on the paper plate.
3. Cut small circles from black paper and paste them on the head for eyes.

COOKING:
CHILD-FRIENDLY TRAIL MIX

Franklin went for a long walk to see if he could find a solution to his problem. By the time he was finished, he was very hungry. Often, when we go shopping with our children, they want everything they see...partly because they may be hungry and partly because they are bored. Make this yummy trail mix and take it along when you go so that your child will have something nutritious to munch on.

You will need: 1 cup unsalted peanuts or other nuts, 1 cup hulled sunflower seeds, 1 cup coconut flakes, 1 cup raisins, 1 cup dried fruit cut into small pieces, a large bowl, and a package of zip-lock plastic bags.

1. Mix together all ingredients in a large bowl.
2. Store in an airtight container or large glass jar with lid. Scoop out a small zip-lock bagful for your child when needed. Makes 5 cups trail mix.

Important tip: You can make an alternative trail mix for very young children who are not old enough to manage nuts and seeds or for those who have allergies. Combine several different types of dry cereals, rounds of Melba toast and pieces of zwieback. Your little ones will enjoy the different shapes and tastes and will be occupied while you shop.

READING:
JOHNNY LION'S BAD DAY

Written by Edith Hurd
Illustrated by Clement Hurd
(USA: Harper Collins Publishers, 1970)

Johnny Lion has a bad cold and he does not like being sick. His parents insist he stay in bed and take his medicine. The medicine tastes horrible and every time he falls asleep, he has terrible nightmares. When his parents bring him a delicious dinner (probably chicken soup...see the recipe on the next page), Johnny Lion tells them about his nightmares and they listen with understanding and reassure him that all will be well. During the night, Johnny dreams he is a big, strong lion and he goes into his parents' room to see if he can wake them with his big roar. His parents let him sleep in their bed for the rest of the night, and in the morning, Johnny is feeling much better. WARNING: if your child is in the habit of wanting to sleep in your bed and you are trying to discourage that, you might want to alter that particular part of the story.

POSITIVE PARENTAL PARTICIPATION NOTE:

Most people don't like to be sick, and children find it especially difficult to be inactive. They need your reassurance that they will get better and that by taking their medicine, not running around, drinking plenty of fluids, etc. they will recover more quickly. Perhaps you could fill a box with small toys and special games...to be opened only when your child is ill...and include an ornate spoon to be used only for medicine.

NOTES:

_____

_____

_____

_____

_____

_____

CRAFTING:
PAPER PLATE LIONS

You will need: 1 paper plate, 1 piece of brown or yellow construction paper, markers or crayons, paste, and scissors.

1. Cut the paper into one-inch wide strips and roll each strip around a marker or crayon to create the curl.
2. Paste one end of one strip to the edge of the plate. Continue with the rest of the strips all around the edge of the plate to form the lion's mane.
3. Using markers or crayons, draw the lion's features.

COOKING:
CHILD-FRIENDLY ALPHABET CHICKEN SOUP

The soup commercial on television says it all...eager, smiling children sitting around the table in a cozy kitchen, mother wearing an apron, stirring a big pot on the stove. The only thing missing is the delicious aroma of homemade soup. With this recipe, you and your child can make that happen in your home.

You will need: 1 qt chicken broth, 2 Tb diced onion, ¼ cup alphabet noodles, 1 cup diced cooked chicken, ½ cup sliced carrots, ½ cup cut green beans, ¼ cup corn kernels, parsley (optional), and a large pot with a cover.

1. In a large pot, mix the broth, onion and noodles and bring to a boil.
2. Lower the heat to simmer and add the chicken, carrots, beans and corn. Simmer with the cover on for 20 minutes, stirring occasionally.
3. Garnish each serving with parsley if you like.
4. Makes about 4-5 cups of soup...refrigerate or freeze what you don't use.

Important tip: You can substitute other vegetables if you like: peas, lima beans, zucchini...use your imagination!

READING:
MADELINE

Written and illustrated by Ludwig Bemelmans
(New York: The Viking Press, 1939)

Madeline is a little girl who lives in a school operated by nuns in Paris, France. Madeline becomes ill one evening and is rushed to the hospital for an emergency appendectomy. The next morning her classmates visit her and are jealous of her situation at the hospital...candy, flowers and lots of attention. That night, the other little girls wake the nuns and pretend to have stomachaches so they will be sent to the hospital.

POSITIVE PARENTAL PARTICIPATION NOTE:

Young children are often frightened when they become ill and have to go to the doctor or to the hospital. Why not visit a hospital with your child one afternoon and walk through some of the halls and have a snack at the cafeteria. If your child ever has to go to the hospital for care or testing, he will feel more comfortable because he has already been there in a non-threatening situation.

NOTES:

_____

_____

_____

_____

_____

_____

_____

_____

_____

_____

_____

CRAFTING:
MAKING GET-WELL CARDS

I'll never forget the letter my son received from the husband of a blind woman. Four-year old Peter had taken part in a church project that was aimed at reaching out to homebound members of the congregation. Peter's card was filled with ribbons, pictures, macaroni and sequins...there was not an inch of blank space left on the card. The man wrote that his wife was overjoyed to feel the different shapes and textures and knew that someone had put a lot of time and effort into making the card for her. *You will need: Construction paper, old magazines, crayons or markers, paste, scissors, ribbons, and buttons.*

1. Let your child choose pictures from old magazines and help him cut them out and paste them on the folded construction paper and add ribbons or buttons.
2. Send the card to a homebound or ill friend or relative.

COOKING:
CHILD-FRIENDLY SWEET-WHEAT BREAD

In the story, Madeline and her friends have bread at every meal. This was (and still is) my children's favorite bread...they loved making it and eating it! *You will need: 2 cups warm milk, 2 packages yeast, ½ cup canola oil, ½ cup honey, 1 egg beaten, ¼ tsp salt, ½ tsp vanilla, ½ cup wheat germ, 5 cups flour, 1 Tb milk, 1 Tb honey, large bowl, and 2 lightly greased loaf pans.*

1. Combine milk and yeast in large bowl and mix well. Then beat in 1 cup of flour.
2. Add canola oil, honey, egg, salt, vanilla and wheat germ and beat well.
3. Add enough flour (about 4 cups) gradually mixing till you can knead the dough.
4. Knead 5-10 minutes till smooth (you can give your child a small piece of his own to work on) keeping a little flour nearby for your hands if the dough is too sticky.
5. Put kneaded dough in lightly greased bowl and cover with clean cloth and let rise for about an hour. Then punch down and shape into loaves and let rise till a finger mark remains when you press a finger into the dough (about ½ hour).
6. Preheat oven to 350 degrees and bake about 25 minutes. Brush tops with milk and honey, if desired, and bake 5 more minutes. Cool on wire racks. Makes 2 regular-size loaves or 4 or 5 mini loaves.

READING:
THE KISSING HAND

Written by Audrey Penn
Illustrated by Ruth Harper and Nancy Leak
(Washington, DC: Child & Family Press, 1993)

Chester Raccoon will be starting kindergarten in the morning and he is very anxious. He confides in his mother and she explains that everyone has to do things they don't want to sometimes. She reassures him that he will enjoy school and tells him there is a secret that she learned from her mother that will help him feel close to her, even when he is away at school. She kisses the inside of his hand and tells him that when he is lonely or needing to be reminded of her love, all he has to do is press his hand to his cheek and think "Mommy loves you" and the kiss will still be there. Chester is completely reassured by this kissing hand secret and he kisses his mother's palm so that she, too, will have a reminder of his love while he is away.

POSITIVE PARENTAL PARTICIPATION NOTE:

A young child is often anxious about the first day of school because it is a new experience and it may be the first time he will be separated from his mother for any length of time. Visiting the facility before school starts will help lessen your child's anxiety. If your child is uncomfortable about being away from you, perhaps you can try Mother Raccoon's suggestion.

NOTES:

_____

_____

_____

_____

_____

_____

_____

CRAFTING:
CLAY HANDPRINTS

Tucked away in an old cedar chest reside many of the treasured keepsakes from when my children were young. Among those are the clay handprints they each made when they were about four years old. Your child can make one just like that.

You will need: One cup of clay (either store-bought or homemade), and one piece of cardboard for the base.

1. Work the clay into a ball; roll it flat…about ½ inch thick.
2. Put the flattened clay on the cardboard and position your child's hand, fingers spread slightly, in the center. Help your child press his hand into the clay.
3. Let the clay dry overnight. Optional: You can varnish it or paint it with clear nail polish. WARNING: Do this outside or with excellent ventilation…this step is not for your child as the fumes are toxic. You can mount the dry handprint on a piece of wood.

COOKING:
CHILD-FRIENDLY THUMBPRINT COOKIES

You will need: 1 cup canola oil, ½ cup honey, 1 egg, 1 tsp vanilla, ½ tsp salt, 3 cups flour, ½ cup jelly or jam, ½ cup sugar in a saucer, cookie sheet, large mixing bowl, and an electric mixer.

1. Preheat oven to 350 degrees while you cream the oil and honey in a large bowl.
2. Beat in the egg and vanilla and then gradually add the flour and salt.
3. Roll a tablespoonful of dough into a ball and then roll it in the saucer of sugar and put on an ungreased cookie sheet, spacing the balls about two inches apart.
4. Press down lightly on each ball with your thumb (or your child's thumb) and fill each depression with jelly or jam.
5. Bake 10 to 12 minutes till cookies are lightly browned.
6. Remove from cookie sheet when cooled. Makes about four dozen.

NOTES:

CHAPTER SIX: "I LIKE MYSELF!"

How to help your child feel good about his body and himself

"**H**ere they come! Here they come!" shouted seven-year old Jason, peering out the window as his aunt, uncle and three cousins walked up the path to the front door. Jason and his four-year old brother, Peter, had been eagerly awaiting this family visit. However, during the flurry of activity when everyone was saying hello, I noticed that little Peter was hanging back. Quickly, I went to him and, squatting down, I asked, 'Honey, is everything OK?" Peter looked up at me tearfully and replied, "Too much hugging and too many

> *"You cannot be lonely if you like the person you're alone with."*
> **Dr. Wayne Dyer**

kisses, Mommy!" "It does feel that way sometimes, doesn't it?" I said. Taking his hand, I continued, "If you don't feel like hugs or kisses, you can just say so. Remember we read *Your Body Belongs To You* the other day. The little boy in that story felt the same way. Why don't you get the Touch and Feel book you made yesterday and show it to your cousins?" Peter's smile returned and he reached out to give me a quick hug and a kiss. "Maybe just one hug and kiss for each person," he exclaimed happily, as he let go of my hand, grabbed the homemade book from the counter, and skipped back to greet the family.

POSITIVE PARENTAL PARTICIPATION NOTE:

Children will feel good about who they are if we encourage them to develop a positive attitude toward their bodies and allow them to see the adults around them show concern, affection and respect for them and for each other. Establishing an atmosphere of comfort and trust enables children to come to us with their questions and concerns. The picture books in this chapter focus on acknowledging the curiosity of young children, encouraging their questions, teaching them the family and safety rules, and giving them positive messages about the human body. As you read the stories with your child and participate positively with him in the craft and cooking activities, many opportunities will arise for honest and open communication. Listen well, and respond with loving understanding…your time and patience will be rewarded, now and in the future. Children who are encouraged at a young age to speak openly and honestly with their parents will be more likely to share concerns and troubles as they grow up.

READING:
THE MIXED-UP CHAMELEON

Written and illustrated by Eric Carle
(New York: HarperCollins Publishers, 1975)

A little green chameleon sat on a leaf and contemplated his existence. He did not think much of himself and felt his life was quite boring and dull. After visiting a zoo, the chameleon believed it would be better to be one of the other animals, but although he was able to become elephant-like, fox-like, etc. (after all, he was a chameleon), these changes did not make him happy. He finally realized that the way he looked originally was perfect for him.

POSITIVE PARENTAL PARTICIPATION NOTE:

Many children are not happy with themselves or comfortable with their bodies…they wish they were taller or older or stronger or smarter or had blond curls like their best friend or straight red hair like the next-door-neighbor. As parents, we need to give our young children positive messages about their looks and their accomplishments on a daily basis. In addition, we need to respect their feelings and applaud their individuality, instead of encouraging them to conform to the norm.

NOTES:

_____
_____
_____
_____
_____
_____
_____
_____
_____
_____
_____

CRAFTING:
CHAMELEON POPSICLE STICK PUPPET

You will need: Plastic wrap, Popsicle stick, glue, construction paper, and scissors.

1. Draw the shape of a chameleon on construction paper (use the illustrations in the book for a model).
2. Leaving about a ½ inch border cut out the inside of the chameleon shape and attach a piece of plastic wrap to the border with glue.
3. Glue the chameleon to the top of the stick.
4. You can see through the plastic wrap…have your child move his puppet over vividly colored surfaces…his chameleon will seem to change color.

COOKING:
CHILD-FRIENDLY NOODLE APPLE CASSEROLE

Just like the chameleon, this pasta dish can change its look from a main dish for lunch, a side dish with dinner, or a dessert or snack, depending on when it is served.

You will need: 4 cups cooked wide noodles, 2 eggs, ¼ cup honey, ½ tsp cinnamon, 1 cup grated apple, ½ cup raisins, 1 Tb margarine or butter, large bowl, and a 2 qt greased casserole dish.

1. In a large bowl, combine eggs, honey and cinnamon and beat well.
2. Stir in apples, raisins, noodles and butter.
3. Pour into a greased casserole dish, cover with aluminum foil, and bake at 400 degrees for 30 minutes.
4. Makes 4 lunch servings or many more side dish, snack or dessert servings.

Important tip: Be careful when you pull away the aluminum foil; there may be a lot of hot steam!

READING:
YOUR BODY BELONGS TO YOU

Written by Cornelia Spelman
Illustrated by Teri Weidner
(Morton Grove, IL: Albert Whitman & Co., 1997)

Using charming illustrations of children of various ethnic backgrounds along with very simple text easily understood by the very young, this book explains what to say and do if someone touches your body when you do not want to be touched. The author makes it clear that a young child should feel empowered to say no, even to a hug or kiss from a family member…we all have moments when we don't feel like being touched.

POSITIVE PARENTAL PARTICIPATION NOTE:

This author has a series of books that address various difficult issues that parents and young children often have to contend with, and she always has a section specifically for the parent that explains the problem and how to deal with it. If a young child does not feel like hugging and kissing every relative who comes to visit, his wishes should be respected. Overriding a young child's feelings in this regard may send him a message that he must obey every adult, no matter what, even if he is being made to feel uncomfortable. In addition, the author makes a distinction between different types of secrets: secrets about touching are never permitted (because any touching that has to be kept a secret is not good touching), whereas pleasant secrets are allowed, such as not telling about a birthday surprise for daddy.

NOTES:

_____

_____

_____

_____

_____

_____

CRAFTING:
TOUCH AND FEEL BOOK

Children definitely enjoy the feel of different textures…you can help your child make his own touch and feel book to help develop that important sense.

You will need: Several pages of construction paper, an assortment of small pieces of fabric and other materials (velvet, silk, wool, cardboard, sandpaper, etc.), paste, scissors, and markers.

1. Fold the pages of construction paper to make a book and staple the folded edge.
2. Paste a different piece of material on each page. Using markers let your child draw a picture incorporating the piece of material (for example: a velvet circle can be the tummy of a teddy bear). Then talk to your child about each picture and write a description of the texture (for example: MY TEDDY BEAR IS SOFT).

COOKING:
CHILD-FRIENDLY PEANUT FINGERS

You will need: 5 slices of bread, ½ cup peanut butter, 2 Tb canola oil, 1 Tb honey, ½ cup minced or flaked coconut, 2 Tb apple juice, double boiler or microwave-safe bowl, a sheet of waxed paper and a cookie sheet.

1. Melt peanut butter, oil, apple juice and honey in double boiler. If you prefer, you can mix these ingredients in a microwave-safe bowl and heat them in the microwave (1 minute at a time on low power), stirring each time.
2. Remove crust from bread and cut each slice into ½ inch fingers.
3. Place crusts and bread fingers on cookie sheet and bake at 250 degrees till dry and light brown. Crush the dried crusts into crumbs and reserve for another recipe.
4. Spread each cooled bread finger with the warm peanut butter mixture and then roll each finger in coconut. Put on wax paper-lined cookie sheet to dry.

Makes about 20 fingers. Store in airtight container in the refrigerator.

READING:
I'M TERRIFIC

Written by Marjorie Weinman Sharmat
Illustrated by Kay Chorao
(New York: Holiday House, 1977)

Jason Everett Bear lives with his mother in the forest. He has grown up with a wonderful opinion of himself...he is terrific and he knows it! The problem is that he is constantly telling his friends how terrific he is and how he always does everything right. His friends ignore him and don't want to be with him so Jason decides to change his ways. After several disappointing attempts, he finally realizes that he is a wonderful bear, but he doesn't need to tell everyone else. His friends enjoy being with him now and everyone is happy.

POSITIVE PARENTAL PARTICIPATION NOTE:

Although Jason had a very good opinion of himself, he was quite conceited about it. We want to help our children develop a high self-esteem...but we also want them to understand that they shouldn't brag about how smart or wonderful they are. When a person is very sure of his true self-worth, he has no need to tell others about his accomplishments or display arrogance or conceit.

NOTES:

_____

_____

_____

_____

_____

_____

_____

_____

_____

_____

CRAFTING:
GOLD-STAR PICTURE

You will need: Package of gold self-stick stars, piece of construction paper, and markers or crayons.

1. Let your child draw a picture of anything that he wants.
2. Your child can use the gold stars to outline what he has drawn or fill in the figures. In addition, he can place gold stars along the edges of the paper to form a frame.

COOKING:
CHILD-FRIENDLY GREEN CLOUD SUPREME (CREAMY CURRIED SPINACH)

Young children often reject vegetables, especially spinach, as unappetizing foods. This recipe may change that tendency!

You will need: 1 (10 oz) package frozen chopped spinach, 1 tsp margarine, 3 Tb sour cream or yogurt, ¼ tsp curry powder, 1 pinch cinnamon, ½ tsp salt, 1 tsp honey, large saucepan, and a pot with cover.

1. In a pot, prepare spinach according to package directions and drain well.
2. In separate saucepan, melt margarine over low heat and blend in remaining ingredients.
3. Add cooked spinach to mixture in pan and toss well to blend.
4. Makes 4 servings.

READING:
WHEN YOU WERE BORN

Written by Dianna Hutts Aston
Illustrated by E.B. Lewis
(Cambridge, MA: Candlewick Press, 2004)

This book is a celebration of the birth and the uniqueness of a child. The mother and father gaze at their baby in wonder. The grandmother sings lullabies and the grandfather holds the infant close to his heart, dreaming of the wonderful future his grandchild will have. The neighborhood children gently play with the baby's toes and their mothers cuddle the new infant, remembering when their children were that small. Even though the rest of the world continues its hectic pace without pause, life for the family with the new baby will never be the same.

POSITIVE PARENTAL PARTICIPATION NOTE:

Young children form their self-image very early on...and parents are the primary contributors to this process. Positive Parental Participation helps a child learn that his parents like him and enjoy being with him...it follows that he will like himself. One of the contributing factors to self-esteem is how we perceive others see us... parents need to interact with their young children in a positive and loving way on a daily basis.

NOTES:

_____

_____

_____

_____

_____

_____

_____

_____

CRAFTING:
BABY COLLAGE

Young children enjoy hearing about when they were "little". You and your child can put together a lovely collage to frame and hang in a place of honor in your home.

You will need: Piece of construction or art paper (suitable for framing), early pictures of your child (in the hospital at birth, in your arms on the way home, being rocked to sleep by a relative, etc.), photo tape, frame, labels, and a fine line marker.

1. Allow your child to choose several pictures of himself as an infant (being held by friends and family, if possible).
2. Arrange them on the art paper and then tell your child the "story" of each picture, writing the words on a label. Affix each label under each picture.
3. Put the collage in a frame and hang in a place of honor in your home.

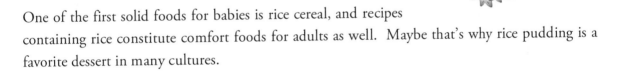

COOKING:
CHILD-FRIENDLY RICE PUDDING

One of the first solid foods for babies is rice cereal, and recipes containing rice constitute comfort foods for adults as well. Maybe that's why rice pudding is a favorite dessert in many cultures.

You will need: 1 cup Basmati rice, ¼ cup honey, ¼ tsp cinnamon, 2½ cups milk, 1 Tb margarine, 1 tsp vanilla, 1 egg yolk, 2 Tb milk, ½ cup raisins, and a pot with a cover.

1. Combine rice, honey, cinnamon, 2½ cups milk, margarine and vanilla in pot. Cover the pot and bring to a boil on medium high.
2. Immediately, turn the heat to very low and simmer gently for 20 minutes.
3. Beat 1 egg yolk with 2 Tb milk. Add this to hot rice slowly, stirring rapidly.
4. Remove from heat. Add raisins.
5. Serve warm or chilled. Refrigerate leftovers in covered container.

READING:
A LION FOR LEWIS

Written and illustrated by Rosemary Wells
(New York: E.P.Dutton, 1982)

Every time little Lewis plays with his older brother and sister, they want him to be the patient (getting shots and being bandaged) or the baby (being diapered and put to sleep). Lewis is unhappy with these roles, but his siblings always ignore his complaints. One day, Lewis finds a lion costume in the attic and puts it on. He convinces his brother and sister that a lion had eaten him, but that since he was able to fight his way free, he deserves to be the king in their next role-playing adventure.

POSITIVE PARENTAL PARTICIPATION NOTE:

How can we help our young children develop the ability to speak up for themselves? Whether it is to request peas instead of lima beans for dinner or to inform us of someone who has been acting inappropriately, our children must feel confident of their worth as individuals. Listening to our children without judging is a key factor in building that level of comfort and confidence.

NOTES:

_____

_____

_____

_____

_____

_____

_____

_____

_____

_____

CRAFTING:
GROCERY BAG LION COSTUME

You will need: Large brown paper grocery bag, yellow, gold or brown yarn, markers, scissors, and paste.

1. Turn the bag upside down and put it over your child so you can mark where his face is.
2. Take the bag off and cut out a circle where his face will show through.
3. Cut the yarn into 5-7 inch strands and paste onto the bag, all around the outside of the circle (this will be the lion's mane).
4. Use the marker to draw the rest of the lion's body on the front of the bag.
5. Cut holes in the sides of the bag for your child's arms to go through.

COOKING:
CHILD-FRIENDLY PUMPKIN BREAD

This is a "quick" bread recipe...no waiting for yeast to rise... and your home will smell divine!

You will need: 1 15 oz can pumpkin (about 2 cups), ¼ cup honey, ¼ cup brown sugar, ½ cup canola oil, 2 eggs, 2½ cups all-purpose flour, 1½ tsp cinnamon, ½ tsp ground cloves, ½ tsp nutmeg, ¼ tsp ground ginger, 2 tsp baking soda, ¼ cup raisins, a large bowl, and a greased 9x5x3 inch loaf pan or 3 mini loaf pans.

1. Combine pumpkin, honey, sugar, oil and eggs and blend well.
2. Add remaining ingredients and blend well.
3. Spoon batter into greased loaf pan.
4. Bake at 350 degrees for 1 hour and cool on wire rack.

Important tip: Your child will enjoy smelling the aroma of the different spices used...if you are able to, you might want to have on hand a real cinnamon stick, a piece of ginger root and some whole cloves and nutmegs so that your child can see where the ground spices come from.

READING:
TOUGH EDDIE

Written by Elizabeth Winthrop
Illustrated by Lillian Hoban
(New York: Dutton, 1985)

Eddie loves to wear his cowboy boots and thick leather belt. He enjoys building with blocks and playing with his friends, Andrew and Philip. Eddie also likes playing with his very own dollhouse, but he keeps it hidden from his friends because he believes they will make fun of him. However, he discovers that his friends would like to play with it also and that they respect him and like him as he is, no matter what he is playing with.

POSITIVE PARENTAL PARTICIPATION NOTE:

If we encourage our young children to pursue their own individual interests…whether or not those interests seem to be the norm, we are telling them that they are likable as they are. Feeling good about oneself and liking oneself are important factors in the development of a good self-image. In addition, a child with a good self-image is less likely to be influenced by peer pressure into doing what he knows is wrong.

NOTES:

_____

_____

_____

_____

_____

_____

_____

_____

_____

_____

CRAFTING:
SHOEBOX DOLLHOUSE

You will need: Large shoebox, old magazines, paste, scissors, wallpaper samples, cardboard, and pipe cleaners (optional).

1. Cut the wallpaper sample to fit the inside "walls" of the shoebox and paste in.
2. Let your child decide what room the shoebox dollhouse will be and look through magazines to find appropriate pictures to furnish it.
3. Help your child cut out the pictures of a bed, chairs, table, TV, etc. and paste them on cardboard and carefully cut along the picture lines. The cardboard will give some stability to the "furniture".
4. You can also cut out people from the magazine (make sure they are appropriate sizes) to inhabit the dollhouse or use pipe cleaners to twist into stick figures.

COOKING:
CHILD-FRIENDLY SWEET POTATO APPLE PIE

Here is an apple pie recipe that is not the "norm"...make it with your child and help celebrate differences!

You will need: 1 unbaked 8 inch piecrust, 1 large sweet potato baked, 2 cups apple (peeled and shredded), 1/8 cup orange or apple juice, ¼ cup light brown sugar plus 2 Tb reserved, ¼ cup coconut flakes, ½ tsp cinnamon, and a large bowl.

1. Peel potato and mash it and mix it with all of the other ingredients (except the 2 Tb of reserved brown sugar).
2. Spread into piecrust and sprinkle with 2 Tb brown sugar.
3. Bake at 350 degrees for about an hour until crust is nicely browned and a toothpick poked in center comes out clean.
4. Cool at least 10 minutes before cutting.
5. Store unused portion in the refrigerator.

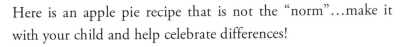

READING:
DID THE SUN SHINE BEFORE YOU WERE BORN?

Written by Sol and Judith Gordon
Illustrated by Vivien Cohen
(New York: Joseph Okpaku Publishing Company, Inc., 1974)

This charmingly illustrated sex education primer addresses many of the questions that young children ask their parents regarding where they came from. The multi-ethnic characters create an appeal to a wide audience and the book contains explanations about how a mother gets pregnant as well as how the baby grows inside of her. More importantly, the book focuses on how special each baby is and how much each child is loved by his parents.

POSITIVE PARENTAL PARTICIPATION NOTE:

Young children ask many questions and parents need to answer them simply and honestly. We want our children to feel comfortable about coming to us with any questions, problems or concerns. If we are embarrassed by their questions or annoyed by their problems or flippant about their concerns, our children will soon learn not to approach us and may either seek out answers and comfort from others or internalize their concerns and become stressed.

NOTES:

_____

_____

_____

_____

_____

_____

_____

_____

_____

CRAFTING:
MAKE A FAMILY TREE

You will need: Large piece of oak tag or heavy construction paper, paste, scissors, several sheets of construction paper in various colors, and pictures of family members (if available).

1. Look through family albums if you have them and talk with your child about the various members of the family and how they are related to him.
2. Draw the outline of a tree on the oak tag. Cut leaf shapes from construction paper and paste them in inverted pyramid fashion with one in the bottom center of the tree's leaves (this will be for your child), one on either side but slightly above (for your child's mother and father), two on either side but slightly above those (for the grandparents), and so on…as far as you can trace your family. For very young children, probably grandparents and great-grandparents are enough to include. If you have photos that you don't mind using, you can paste them in, labeling each with the appropriate name. Otherwise, you and your child can draw the faces.
3. Hang this lovely keepsake in a place of honor in your home; celebrating your child's roots…a great boost to his self-image!

COOKING:
CHILD-FRIENDLY SUNSHINE CAKE

You will need: 2 Tb margarine or butter, ½ cup brown sugar, 1 large can pineapple slices (9 slices with juice), 4 eggs, ½ cup white sugar, 1½ cups flour, ¼ tsp salt, 1 tsp baking powder, 9 inch lightly greased baking pan, electric mixer, and a large bowl.

1. Melt margarine in pan, spread with brown sugar and top with 9 pineapple slices.
2. In large bowl, beat eggs with electric mixer till thick, gradually adding sugar and ½ cup pineapple juice. Then add flour, salt and baking powder and mix till smooth.
3. Pour mixture over pineapple slices and bake at 325 degrees for one hour.
4. Cool in pan and then invert onto serving plate. Each pineapple is like a little sun!

READING:
SLOPPY KISSES

Written by Elizabeth Winthrop
Illustrated by Anne Burgess
(USA: Macmillan Publishing Co., Inc., 1980)

Emmy Lou's loving family is not ashamed to show how much they love each other. However, when a school friend tells her that kissing is just for babies, Emmy Lou begins to question the way her family shows their love. For several days, Emmy Lou refuses to allow her father to kiss her goodbye at school, and she won't let her parents kiss her when they come to say goodnight to her. Although she is very unhappy, she does not realize why, but her wise and loving parents do. When Emmy Lou cannot get to sleep one night, her parents sit and talk to her and finally just give her a loving kiss and hug. Emmy Lou realizes that this is what she has been missing and she is no longer ashamed to have her father kiss her goodbye at school.

POSITIVE PARENTAL PARTICIPATION NOTE:

Peer pressure is a very powerful influence, often with negative consequences. Children can reject it only if they have a very strong sense of self-confidence and the knowledge that they are worthwhile individuals and entitled to say no or disagree with what someone else says they should do. Emmy Lou's parents respected her temporary wish to refrain from kissing...the respect that they showed her enabled Emmy Lou to believe in herself and make her own decision to ignore her school friend's advice.

NOTES:

_____

_____

_____

_____

_____

_____

CRAFTING:
PAPER BAG PIG

You will need: Small brown paper lunch bag, marker, scissors, construction paper, paste, and 4 pieces of string (or ribbon) about 12 inches each.

1. Draw the face of a pig near the fold at the top of the bag (or cut eyes, ears, snout and whiskers from construction paper and paste on).
2. Cut the entire area of the bag into thin strips below where the neck will be
3. Tie a string around the neck very tightly. Pull a few strands on each side of the bag (these are the arms) and cut to arm length and tie a string at each wrist.
4. Tie a string at the waist…it looks like the pig is wearing a skirt…if you want to make a "boy" pig…separate the strips below the waist into legs and tie at the ankles.
5. Cut a thin strip of construction paper and roll it around a pencil…when it unrolls a little you can paste it on the back of the bag for the pig's curly tail.

COOKING:
CHILD-FRIENDLY CURLIQUE PASTA BAKE

There are several types of pasta that are curly, just like a little pig's tail.

You will need: 1 lb box pasta, 8 oz shredded mozzarella, ¼ cup Parmesan cheese, 16 oz of ricotta cheese (you can substitute cottage cheese), 1 egg, 1 Tb parsley, 1 qt spaghetti sauce, a mixing bowl, and a 3 qt casserole dish.

1. Cook pasta according to directions on box and drain.
2. Mix cheeses, egg, and parsley in a bowl.
3. In the casserole dish, layer sauce, pasta, cheese, sauce, pasta, cheese.
4. Bake at 350 degrees for 45 minutes. This makes about 8 servings.

READING:
STRANGER DANGER

Written by Cynthia MacGregor
Photos by Seth Dinnerman and Phyllis Picardi
(New York: PowerKids Press, 1999)

Although this book is geared toward elementary school age children, the photos will appeal to younger children as well. If necessary, you can change some of the words so that the text is more appropriate for a younger child. Each topic covered helps explain why it is important to be careful around strangers and how even a young child can protect himself in various situations. For example, one photo shows a young boy running and the text explains that if a stranger approaches you and asks you to help find her lost pet, you must remember that it is a stranger and you shouldn't believe what she tells you. The child is encouraged to trust his own feelings and run away yelling.

POSITIVE PARENTAL PARTICIPATION NOTE:

We need to equip our young children with confidence by giving them the knowledge of situations that might arise and the appropriate responses for them in those situations. This knowledge will empower your child and help him develop a strong self-image.

NOTES:

_____
_____
_____
_____
_____
_____
_____
_____
_____
_____

CRAFTING:
CLAY FINGER MASK PUPPETS

You will need: Hardening clay (either store-bought or from the non-edible recipe section), small glass or jar, and cover-ups for work surface.

1. For the face, break off a lump of clay and roll into a golf-sized ball. Flatten it and cut out a circle with the small glass.
2. Take two more marble-sized lumps of clay and roll each into a coil long enough to go around the clay circle. Moisten with water and press each around the circle's edge.
3. Stick small pieces of clay to the face of the circle for eyes, nose and mouth.
4. For the finger loops, take a marble-size lump of clay and roll it into a coil twice as long as your index finger. Flatten the coil and turn in each end so you will have two circles. Attach to the "neck" of the face circle by moistening with water. When the clay has hardened, your child will be able to put two fingers through the loops and make the puppet walk, run or dance. You can add yarn for hair, and then paint it, if desired.

COOKING:
CHILD-FRIENDLY PASTA WITH FRESH PESTO

You will need: 1 cup minced fresh parsley, ¾ cup minced fresh basil (or ½ cup dried crushed), 1 tsp salt, ½ cup olive oil, ½ lb uncooked pasta, grated Parmesan cheese, and a blender or a food processor.

1. Grind the herbs and salt in food processor or blender.
2. Add oil and mix till smooth.
3. Cook pasta according to package directions. Drain and toss with green sauce and sprinkle each serving with Parmesan cheese, if desired.

Makes 4 servings.

READING:
LET'S TALK ABOUT SAYING NO

Written by Joy Berry
Illustrated by Maggie Smith
(New York: Scholastic, Inc., 1996)

In this book, a little girl named Tonya learns when it is appropriate to say no and when it is not. For example, when her mother asks her to pick up her toys, Tonya should not say no. However, when her friend encourages Tonya to eat the cookies her mother had told them not to, Tonya should feel comfortable saying no. If her father tells her it is time for bed, Tonya needs to respond affirmatively. But she should say no if someone tells her that she has to feel a certain way about something even though she doesn't. The multi-ethnic illustrations are bright and appealing and the various situations in which Tonya finds herself will be easy for young children to relate to.

POSITIVE PARENTAL PARTICIPATION NOTE:

Parents often joke about the "terrible twos" and the propensity of young children from that age onward to use the word "no". No, however, is a very important word for our young children to learn...we must help teach them when to use it. Children who like themselves will be more confident in using the word "no" at the appropriate times.

NOTES:

_____

_____

_____

_____

_____

_____

_____

_____

_____

CRAFTING:
YES AND NO FLASHCARDS

Help your child "know" when to say "no" by playing a game with these.

You will need: Several sheets of heavy weight construction paper, old magazines, paste, markers, and scissors.

1. Cut the paper into uniform rectangles, about 4 inches x 6 inches or larger.
2. Decide what situations you would like to represent on the flashcards. For example: Should we share toys with friends; should we help pick up and put away toys; do we say please and thank you at the dinner table; do we talk to strangers; should we tell a trusted adult if someone makes us uncomfortable?
3. Look through some old magazines with your child for pictures that you could use on the flashcards. For example: toys, food, people.
4. Cut out the pictures and paste each on a separate card. On the back, write the scenario question you want to illustrate.
5. Take turns with your child choosing flashcards and answering the questions with a yes or no. You will have to be the "official" question reader for the game.

COOKING:
CHOCOLATE CHIP COOKIES

Here is a wonderful recipe for those chocolate chip cookies that Tonya had to wait for…perhaps your child can have a special friend over to share this treat. *You will need: 1 cup canola oil, 1 cup light brown sugar, 1 egg, 1 tsp vanilla, ½ tsp baking powder, 1¾ cup flour, ½ tsp baking soda, ½ tsp salt, 1 cup quick oats, 1 cup chocolate chips, greased baking sheets, 2 bowls, electric beaters, and wire racks.*

1. In a large bowl, beat the oil, sugar, egg and vanilla with electric beater.
2. In another bowl, mix the flour, salt, baking powder and baking soda and add gradually to the creamed mixture.
3. Stir in oats and chocolate chips and drop by teaspoonfuls onto greased baking sheets.
4. Bake 12 to 14 minutes at 350 degrees. Cool on wire racks. Makes 5-6 dozen.

READING:
TELL ME MY STORY, MAMA

Written by Deb Lund
Illustrated by Hiroe Nakata
(USA: HarperCollins Publishers, 2004)

When her mother is expecting a baby, a little girl enjoys hearing about what happened when she was growing inside her mother. It is obvious that she has heard this same story many times before because she already knows what is going to happen and she prompts her mother to relate various special times during the pregnancy.

POSITIVE PARENTAL PARTICIPATION NOTE:

Most young children are curious about where they came from and how they got here. In addition, they want to know that they are an important part of their family: eagerly anticipated and joyfully accepted once they arrived. We can help our children develop a positive self-image by relaying stories about their beginnings and showing them how special they are to us.

NOTES:

_____

_____

_____

_____

_____

_____

_____

_____

_____

_____

_____

_____

CRAFTING:
COLOR FOOD COLLAGE

You will need: Large piece of poster board or construction paper, old magazines, paste, scissors, and markers.

1. Help your child look through the magazines to find pictures of foods. Cut them out and separate them into different piles, one for each color.
2. Use a marker to divide the poster board into as many sections as you need…one section for each color…use a marker to put a colored dot in each section and write the color word in that section also.

Paste each food in the correct section according to color (for example: tomatoes would go in the red section, peas in the green, etc.).

COOKING:
CHILD-FRIENDLY COLORFUL SUMMER FRUIT CRISP

You can use your imagination when assembling the fruits…how many different colors will there be in this delicious and healthful dessert?

You will need: 5 cups mixed summer fruit, washed and then sliced if necessary (peaches, plums, apricots, strawberries, blueberries, etc.), ¼ cup white sugar, ¼ cup orange juice, 1 tsp lemon juice, 3 Tb flour (for fruit), ¼ cup flour (for topping), 2 cups rolled oats, ¼ cup brown sugar, 1 tsp cinnamon, ¼ cup margarine, softened, a greased 9x13 inch pan, and 2 large bowls.

1. In a large bowl, gently toss fruit with white sugar, orange juice and lemon juice.
2. Sprinkle with 3 Tb flour, toss gently again and spread in the greased pan.
3. In another bowl, mix oats, brown sugar, cinnamon and the remaining flour. Then add margarine and mix till crumbly.
4. Sprinkle crumbly mixture over fruit.
5. Bake 20-25 minutes at 375 degrees until fruit is tender and topping is golden brown. Serve warm or at room temperature. Serves 12.

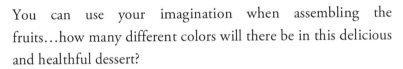

READING:
THE RIGHT TOUCH

Written by Sandy Kleven
Illustrated by Jody Bergsma
(Bellevue, WA: Illumination Arts Publishing Company, 1997)

A mother tells her young son a story about a little girl who was tricked by a neighbor whose intentions were to sexually abuse her. Using charming illustrations and a simple, easy to understand text, this book focuses on helping young children identify inappropriate touching. In addition, it spells out clearly just how a young child should respond to that type of situation.

POSITIVE PARENTAL PARTICIPATION NOTE:

As parents, one of our main responsibilities is to keep our children safe. Because we cannot always be with our children, we must educate them so that when they are in school, out playing with friends, home alone with the babysitter or visiting with relatives, they will be prepared to say "no" when a situation makes them uncomfortable. When parents approach the issue in a loving, non-judgmental and understanding way, as did the mother in the story, their child will be more likely to feel he can come to them and tell them anything.

NOTES:

_____

_____

_____

_____

_____

_____

_____

_____

_____

_____

CRAFTING:
PAPER DOLLS WITH CLOTHES

This activity might help serve as a springboard for a discussion on what parts of our body are very private (those covered by our bathing suit). *You will need: Old magazines, cardboard, paste, scissors, construction paper, tape, and an envelope in which to store the pieces.*

1. Look through the magazines with your child and help him find a suitable picture of a person (man, woman or child) that he would like to use as the model for the paper doll (or, you can just draw one, about 5 to 8 inches high).
2. Cut out the picture and paste it on a piece of cardboard. Then carefully cut off the excess cardboard.
3. Turn the paper doll over and use a marker to draw a face and bathing suit.
4. Now you can help your child draw appropriately sized clothing on the construction paper (or find clothing in the magazines). Cut them out and use them to dress the doll, attaching with tape. Store all the pieces in an envelope.

COOKING:
CHILD-FRIENDLY TEA PARTY JAM BARS

I can remember my own children arranging their dolls and stuffed animals around the table as the only guests at an impromptu tea party...these bars would be perfect for just such a party...maybe your child will invite his new paper doll. *You will need: 2 cups flour, ¾ cup sugar, 1 cup ground pecans (or other nuts), ½ cup margarine (softened), 1 egg, 10 oz jar raspberry jam (or other jam or jelly), large bowl, a lightly greased 8 inch baking pan and an electric mixer.*

1. In a large bowl, combine all ingredients except jam. Beat till well mixed.
2. Press all but 1½ cups of the mixture into the pan. Spread jam over the top, almost to the edge. (You can heat the jam a bit in the microwave to make it easier to spread) Crumble reserved topping over jam and press down gently.
3. Bake at 350 degrees for 40-50 minutes till lightly browned.
4. Cool completely before cutting into bars.

READING:
IT'S MY BODY

Written by Lory Freeman
Illustrated by Carol Deach
(Seattle, WA: Parenting Press, Inc., 1982)

The main character in this story is a little girl who is comfortable with the idea that her body belongs to her. Although she is happy to "share her body" when she holds a friend's hand or sits on her grandmother's lap, she understands that she has the right to say "no" to any touching that makes her feel uncomfortable or unhappy. The author provides several commonplace scenarios where comfortable or uncomfortable touching may occur and illustrates the child's assertive, yet reasonable response.

POSITIVE PARENTAL PARTICIPATION NOTE:

As parents, we must teach our young children to make decisions about sharing their bodies and help them learn to communicate these decisions to others. By respecting their feelings, we encourage our children to become confident in how they feel…if, for example, we force them to "kiss Aunt Helen" or endure excessive tickling from an older sibling, we are teaching them that they do not have a right to control their own bodies and that others can "touch" them, even if they are uncomfortable or unhappy about the situation. By empowering our children with assertive responses, we are taking a vital step in protecting our children against sexual abuse.

NOTES:

_____
_____
_____
_____
_____
_____

CRAFTING:
FINGER PUPPETS FOR ROLE-PLAYING

"Don't touch me! I don't like it!" "No, I won't touch you! I don't want to!" How can we help empower our young children to respond like this when necessary? Role-playing is an excellent way and puppets are the perfect medium.

You will need: Cardboard, felt or heavy paper, glue, and scissors.

1. Cut several figures from cardboard, felt or heavy paper. At least one should be a child figure and at least one should be an adult figure.
2. Glue on features cut from felt or paper (eyes, nose, mouth, etc.) or use a marker. Add details for clothing (buttons, belt, etc.).
3. Make a ring of heavy paper that your child's finger will fit inside and glue to the back of each puppet.
4. Enact several scenes with your child while both of you are using the puppets. Then let your child use both puppets by himself.

COOKING:
CHILD-FRIENDLY "BETTER THAN FAST FOOD" CHICKEN FINGERS

You will need: 1 lb boneless skinless chicken breasts, 1 Tb soy sauce or Bragg's Aminos, 1 tsp garlic powder, 2 tsp dry oregano, 1 tsp dry basil, ½ cup crushed dried breadcrumbs, lightly greased baking pan, bowl, and 2 paper lunch bags.

1. Cut chicken into ¾ inch wide strips about the length of a finger and place in a bowl with soy sauce or Bragg's Aminos.
2. Put spices in one paper bag and breadcrumbs in the second bag.
3. Put the chicken in the spice bag and shake well. Then transfer to the breadcrumb bag and shake well again, pressing the crumbs into the chicken strips. Your child will love being the "official" bag-shaker!
4. Put chicken fingers on greased pan and bake at 375 degrees for 8-10 minutes until crisp. Serves 4.

READING:
IF YOU WERE BORN A KITTEN

Written by Marion Dane Bauer
Illustrated by JoEllen Mcallister Stammen
(New York: Aladdin Paperbacks, 2001)

Large, true-to-life illustrations and a clear and simple text help describe the first moments of life for many different animals. The last few pages are devoted to the eager anticipation of a human couple as they await the birth of a new baby and then enjoy its arrival.

POSITIVE PARENTAL PARTICIPATION NOTE:

Young children need to know how special they are and how much their parents want them and love them. This knowledge helps a child feel good about himself...an important building block in the development of a high self-esteem.

NOTES:

_____

_____

_____

_____

_____

_____

_____

_____

_____

_____

_____

_____

_____

_____

_____

CRAFTING:
CLAY FAMILIES

You and your child can use one of the clay recipes in the non-edible recipe section for this project or you can use store-bought clay.

You will need: Clay, cover-ups for work surface, and utensils (like a plastic comb or fork, butter knife, etc.) to help mark the features.

1. Talk to your child and decide what family he wants to model…his own or an animal family.
2. Work with the clay by molding one piece or attaching several small pieces together to create each body of the members of the family.
3. When the clay hardens (several hours or several days, depending on the type of clay) you can help your child paint his figures with non-toxic tempera paints.

COOKING:
CHILD-FRIENDLY SWEET RAISIN IRISH SODA BREAD

Lovely to make around St. Patrick's Day…or anytime!

You will need: 2 cups flour, 1 tsp baking powder, ½ tsp baking soda, ¼ tsp salt, 4 Tb margarine, 1 beaten egg (reserve 1 Tb), ¾ cup buttermilk or sour milk, ¼ cup raisins, 2 Tb honey, a large bowl, and a greased baking sheet.

1. In the large bowl, combine flour, baking powder, baking soda and salt.
2. Cut in margarine till mixture looks like coarse crumbs.
3. Combine raisins, 1 beaten egg (minus the 1 Tb) and buttermilk; add to flour mixture and stir till moistened.
4. On lightly floured surface, knead dough gently for 1 minute.
5. On greased baking sheet, shape dough into a 6-inch round loaf.
6. Cut a 4-inch cross, ¼ inch deep, on the top.
7. Brush with reserved tablespoon of egg.
8. Bake at 375 degrees for 35 minutes till golden.
9. Cool on rack. Serves 16 (or less, because everyone will want seconds and thirds).

READING:
ONE OF THE PROBLEMS OF EVERETT ANDERSON

Written by Lucille Clifton
Illustrated by Ann Grifalconi
(New York: Henry Holt and Company, 2001)

A little boy named Everett is concerned about his school friend, Greg. It seems that Greg comes to school with bruises every day and is always very sad. When Everett asks him what is bothering him, Greg says that he can't tell. Everett confides in his own sister and mother and he believes that perhaps now that he has told his mother, things will get better for Greg.

POSITIVE PARENTAL PARTICIPATION NOTE:

Young children can be very perceptive and we need to give them the tools so that they can not only protect themselves, but can also be helpful to others who may be experiencing problems. If we can develop a high degree of trust with our children, they will come to us with their concerns and worries. How can we do this? We must be consistently non-judgmental and love our children unconditionally. This does not mean letting them do whatever they please or refraining from setting limits and rules.

NOTES:

_____

_____

_____

_____

_____

_____

_____

_____

_____

CRAFTING:
A STORY BOOK OF FRIENDS

You will need: Several sheets of construction paper, camera, tape, marker, and a stapler.

1. Fold the sheets of construction paper in half to form a book and staple along the left side.
2. Help your child obtain photos of his friends (and teachers, pets, etc.). Perhaps he can have several friends over to play (or have a tea party…see the preceding projects) and you (or he) can take pictures of the guests. Attach one photo to each page and ask your child to tell you something about that friend while you write it.

COOKING:
CHILD-FRIENDLY BANANA BRAN MUFFINS

These highly nutritious muffins make a wonderful snack, or team with a vegetable salad or soup for a terrific lunch!

You will need: 1 cup whole wheat flour, 1½ tsp baking powder, ¼ tsp baking soda, ½ tsp cinnamon, 1 cup oat bran, 3 Tb milk, 1 egg, ¼ cup canola oil, 1 cup mashed banana, ½ cup raisins, 1 cup applesauce, 1 tsp honey, large bowl, and a lightly greased 12-cup muffin tin.

1. In a large bowl, combine dry ingredients and mix well.
2. Add milk, egg, applesauce and oil and blend together.
3. Stir in raisins and mashed banana.
4. Spoon batter into muffin cups and bake at 375 degrees for about 20 minutes.
5. Cool well before serving. Makes 12 regular-size muffins.

NOTES:

CONCLUSION: "TELL ME ONE MORE STORY, PLEASE!"

How six simple factors and the secret ingredient can build high self-esteem for your children and create balance and harmony for the entire family

Mary, **Meagan** and Marc quickly finish their breakfast, eager to hear about the adventures of *Clifford, The Big Red Dog* by Norman Bridwell. After settling comfortably on the colorful pillows in the story corner, the four-year old triplets eagerly turn their smiling faces towards their mother as she begins to read. When the story is over, all three children clamor, "Tell us one more story, please!" But then Marc interjects, "Can we get a dog?" Their mother listens attentively and respectfully during the lively discussion that ensues as the three preschoolers share their thoughts about what fun it would be to have a dog. Since they live in a small apartment, their mother suggests that perhaps they might be able to keep a smaller and less demanding animal, such as a turtle or some fish, and she offers to take them to the library where they might find some books about alternative pets. Meanwhile, she encourages them to move to the table in the kitchen where she helps her children make paper plate dogs, pasting spots of different sizes and colors onto the plates to individualize their creations. Meagan decides that her paper plate looks like the turtle she may want to have as a pet, so her mother helps her add a head, tail and feet cut from green construction paper. When the children are finished with their craft project, their mother praises each one and hangs all the plates on a special bulletin board. Later, after the promised trip to the library where they each chose a book about a pet they might be able to keep, the children join their mother in making animal-shaped cookies, each taking turns with measuring and mixing the ingredients. In the evening, the triplets get ready for bed, eagerly anticipating the bedtime story they will hear about Frizzy, the turtle.

What is the recipe for building self-esteem in a young child? What ingredients must you add to your child's day to insure he will grow up with a positive self-image? We can successfully develop high self-esteem in young children by teaching them the importance of mastering tasks and skills, by encouraging them to value their own strengths and qualities, by helping them to feel loved, valued and accepted, by teaching them to express their feelings in a constructive manner, by helping them to acknowledge and cope with their fears and lastly, by encouraging them to develop a positive attitude towards their bodies and themselves. **Positive Parental Participation is the "secret" ingredient that must be added to those six factors.** When you spend time with your child in a joyful and loving manner, you are cementing those building blocks of self-esteem.

The program I developed uses a simple schedule that provides a balanced and harmonious day for young children. In the appendix you will find an hour-by-hour schedule that incorporates the story reading, craft project and cooking experience. Most children thrive when daily routines are put into place because, when they know what to expect, their stress level is lowered. In fact, creating a daily schedule is often the first order of business after observing the family on the popular Nanny shows. You will be amazed at the change in the atmosphere at home from frenzied chaos to calm orderliness by just implementing the simple routines I used successfully with my kindergarten students, my day-care toddlers and my own children as they were growing up. More importantly, your young child will be developing a positive self-image, greeting each new day with curiosity and anticipation and, perhaps, the words, "Tell me one more story, please!"

NOTES:

APPENDIX A
MY SUCCESSFUL ROUTINE (TRY IT, YOU'LL LIKE IT!)

Although we live in an age that encourages personal expression and creativity, I believe very strongly that young children (in fact most children of all ages and adults as well) benefit immensely from living and working in an atmosphere of structure and routines. This is not to say that rigid adherence to set rules should be the order of the day. It is extremely important, when dealing with all human beings of any age, to be flexible. However, my experience has shown me that when young children are aware of what is going to happen, they can relax and enjoy the activities.

Each day with the children (my own when they were very young, the youngsters in my pre-K and kindergarten classes, and my day-care group) revolved around a particular book that was read during story-time and different activities that were planned (music/rhythms, science/math, arts/crafts) which related to that story. Although the story and activities would change, the routines remained constant, and the children came to expect and look forward to them. In addition to the story and activities, the schedule allowed for breakfast, snack-time and lunch (feeding children is VERY important and can be a great tool for learning and socialization) and naptime (we all need some quiet time in the day)...all in an atmosphere of love and approval. These routines can be applied to a family with one or more toddlers, as well as a home day care. **Of course, each of you will make whatever modifications are necessary to individualize the program for your own unique situation and child.**

6:30am to 7:30am: GETTING READY FOR THE DAY
My own children awoke around this time, washing, going to the bathroom, brushing teeth, getting dressed - all these things with or without help depending on the age.

7:30am to 8:30am: BREAKFAST
Many health experts and nutritionists talk about the importance of a good breakfast. I found that to be very true, and it was not only an excellent beginning for the day from the standpoint of nutrition, but also a wonderful way to encourage positive socialization skills. Each child had his own special place at the table. French toast, pancakes, scrambled eggs, or cereal were some of the favorite meals served; it is amazing how well even the fussiest child will eat when he or she sees others enjoying the food. Of course, I also believe that the happy and relaxed atmosphere was certainly conducive to their good appetites.

8:30am to 9:15am: STORY-TIME

Anytime is a good time for a story and I agree with all the early childhood experts who believe that early exposure to reading is extremely helpful in insuring that children will grow up to love books. Each day I would choose a book and would base the entire day's activities on the theme of that book. For instance, on a snowy winter day I might choose *The Mitten* by Alvin Tresselt. I would gather the children in a semi-circle around me, making sure that all could see the pictures as I read the story. During the reading of the story, I would point out certain items on a page and ask questions, trying to draw the children into a more active role in the storytelling. After the book was finished, we would have a discussion about the story (you would be surprised how verbal 2, 3, and 4 year-olds can be if they feel comfortable).

9:15am to 9:30am: MUSIC AND RHYTHMS

Children love to move and, after sitting quietly (or comparatively so) for the story, it was time for some activity. Sometimes we would stand and form a circle for circle games such as Hokey Pokey or London Bridge and other times we would imitate trains or animals depending on the book we had read that morning. On the day we read *The Mitten*, we pretended to be snowflakes being blown by the wind and falling to the ground. The piano, an auto-harp, or a cassette tape or CD can be used to accompany the children's movements.

9:30am to 10:15am: ARTS AND CRAFTS

Expressing oneself through art is a vehicle for creativity. Children of all ages take pride in creating their own works of art. For the very young, tearing paper and pasting it is great fun. Older children can use scissors and be more precise. Using paint, crayons, chalk or other media to create their own pictures is always enjoyed by young children. The activity following the reading of *The Mitten*, for example, used different size and color snowflakes pasted on a large sheet of construction paper. In this way, the art activity also became a math lesson (and with young children, most fun activities can do dual duty by also providing real lessons in numbers, letters, history, etc.).

10:15am to 10:30am: MORNING SNACK

Young children need to be reminded to drink during the day...sometimes they get so busy playing they don't realize they are thirsty. The morning snack-time provides the perfect opportunity for juice, milk or water and fruit, crackers or cheese.

10:30am to 11:30am: FREE PLAY

Weather permitting, young children love to be outside. Providing a safe environment for them to play outside is very important. Sandbox, climbing apparatus, balls and other sports equipment scaled to their size will help enhance their time outside. If the weather is inclement, indoor free play can include table games (puzzles, art), wooden or other types of blocks, pretend play areas (such as make-believe stove, fridge, dress up clothes), and, of course, books.

11:30am to 12:00pm: COOKING EXPERIENCE

Cooking is a multi-faceted activity that helps young children learn math and science concepts in addition to increasing their sense of self-worth. On the day we read *The Mitten*, for example, we made homemade hot cocoa to enjoy with our lunch.

12:00pm to 12:45pm: LUNCH

After washing up, the children would again gather around the table, each in their appointed place, to enjoy a nutritious lunch consisting of items like soup and sandwich, fish sticks and fruit, or meatballs and spaghetti. The meal was another opportunity for socialization, and many lessons in good manners and courteous behavior were learned. In addition, math was often brought into the picture as we would discuss how the sandwich was cut into two halves or that there was one plate of spaghetti, two meatballs, three crackers, four apple slices and five grapes at every place.

12:45pm to 2:00pm: NAPTIME

Getting enough rest is as important to having a good day as is eating good food and exercising. Many children are resistant to naps because they feel they have not "done enough" during the day or are missing out on something. Perhaps because I expected them to take a nap or perhaps because they had had a very full morning, every child I ever cared for (my own and others) was content to go to sleep in the afternoon. Sometimes I played soft classical music; sometimes I read a short story as they settled down on their individual blankets or mats.

2:00pm to 3:00pm: FREE PLAY

As the children awoke from their naps, they would use the bathroom, wash up and choose from the indoor toys and games (puzzles, books, blocks, etc.). Weather permitting, outside playtime was also an option. After all, these are young children, and most of their time should be playtime (which for young children is also learning time). I think, however, the key thought is "free play", not "free for all"…children who aimlessly run through the house with no direction at all are usually unhappy children and often get into trouble.

3:00pm to 3:15pm: AFTERNOON SNACK

A light snack of fruit and crackers, vegetable sticks and cheese or toast with a little peanut butter and jelly teamed with milk, juice or water will provide your child with something nutritious until dinner is served. With a little advance planning, you can insure that your child isn't munching on some high-calorie, preservative-loaded, lacking-in-nutrition treat.

During my "day care" years, 3:30pm was the end of the day. Similarly, when I was teaching kindergarten and Head Start, the day ended at 3:00pm. For the parent of a toddler, perhaps your child can help in the dinner preparation in some way, like putting out napkins. Another option is having a longer free playtime till dinner is ready. For those whose day care children remain longer, another round of story and art activity can be provided.

NOTES:

_____
_____
_____
_____
_____
_____
_____
_____
_____
_____
_____
_____
_____
_____
_____
_____
_____
_____
_____

APPENDIX B
NON-EDIBLE RECIPES

You can always buy clay and paints at the store. However, it is quite economical to make your own and it is definitely fun to do it with your child, as well. In addition, there are so many chemicals added to many of the store-bought items, you might like the benefit of mixing the ingredients yourself so the clay and paints are preservative and additive-free.

CLAY DOUGH

This clay must be moistened with water before the pieces will stick together. After several days, this clay dries to a stiff, hard finish. When dry, it can be painted.

You will need: 1½ cups flour, ½ cup salt, ¼ cup vegetable oil, ½ cup water, mixing bowl, and a spoon.

1. Mix flour and salt in bowl.
2. Slowly stir in water and oil.
3. Squeeze the mixture for 3-4 minutes, until it feels like clay.
4. Moisten your hands with water and continue to squeeze if the mixture breaks apart.
5. Store unused clay in a plastic bag or airtight container in the refrigerator.
6. Add a little more flour if it becomes too sticky.

CLAY #2

You will need: 1 cup of flour, ½ cup of salt, ½ cup of hot tap water, and a bowl.

1. Combine flour and salt in the bowl.
2. Pour in the hot water and stir well.
3. Knead the dough on a floured surface for a few minutes.
4. This dough rolls out nicely to make ornaments, pendants and refrigerator magnets.
5. To save the creation, air dry from 1-5 days or bake at 200 degrees for 2 hours on a cookie sheet.
6. Store unused clay in a plastic bag or airtight container in the fridge for up to one week.

TEMPERA PAINT

You will need: Powdered tempera paint (available in art supply stores), water, liquid starch, several small containers with lids, and Popsicle sticks.

1. Pour a small amount of powdered tempera paint into the container.
2. Stir in enough water to make a creamy mixture.
3. Add a few drops of liquid starch.
4. This paint works well with brushes or Q-tips.
5. To make a watercolor wash, put some water in another container, add several drops of the tempera paint and mix.

"EDIBLE" FINGERPAINT

Here is a finger paint that is great for the youngest painters…it is finger-licking good! You might divide the portion you make and save half of it in the refrigerator for snack-time. *You will need: 1 box of instant pudding mix (vanilla for white, chocolate for brown, strawberry for pink, etc.), 1½ cups of milk, large bowl, and a wire whisk.*

1. Mix the pudding and milk in a large bowl until it thickens.
2. Place a few spoonfuls in a bowl, give your child a piece of finger paint paper (freezer paper works well), cover your child's clothing with an old shirt or apron and the work surface with plastic sheeting or newspapers…and have some fun!

BUBBLEBLOWING LIQUID

If your child doesn't like to take a bath, mix up a batch of this and let him blow bubbles while he is in the tub…he'll never want the bath to end! *You will need: ¼ cup baby shampoo, one cup of water, container with lid, and wire or pipe cleaners.*

1. Gently mix baby shampoo and water in container.
2. Bend the wire or pipe cleaner to form a loop on top (big loop=big bubbles).
3. Dip the loop into the container, remove carefully and blow through the loop.

You can look around the house for other implements that might be fun to blow through (nothing made of glass) that would be safe to use in the tub.

REFERENCES

Burros, Marian. (1978), *Pure & Simple: Delicious Recipes for Additive Free Cooking.* New York: William Morrow and Company, Inc.

Butler, Shelley and Kratz, Deb. (1999), *Field Guide to Parenting: A Comprehensive Handbook of Great Ideas, Advice, Tips and Solutions for Parenting Children Ages One to Five.* Worcester, MA: Chandler House Press.

Church, Lisa. (1998), *Everyday Creative Play.* Minneapolis, MN: Fairview Press.

Cole, Ann, Haas, Carolyn, Heller, Elizabeth, and Weinberger, Betty. (1978), *Children are Children are Children: An Activity Approach to Exploring Brazil, France, Iran, Japan, Nigeria and the U.S.S.R.* Boston, MA: Little, Brown and Company.

Cutright, Melitta. (1992), *Growing Up Confident: How to Make Your Child's Early Years Learning Years.* New York: Doubleday.

Dahlstrom, Carol Field (editor). (2001), *501 Fun-to-Make Family Crafts.* Des Moines, Iowa: Better Homes and Gardens Books.

Dargatz, Jan. (1991), *52 Simple Ways to Build Your Child's Self-Esteem and Confidence.* Nashville, TN: Oliver-Nelson.

Earth Works Group, (1989), *50 Simple Things You Can Do To Save The Earth.* Berkeley, CA: Earthworks Press.

Forisha, William. (1988), *Creating a Good Self Image in Your Child.* Chicago, IL: Contemporary Books.

Greenberg, Marian. (1979), *Your Children Need Music.* New Jersey: Prentice Hall.

Hauser, Jill Frankel. (1993), *Growing Up Reading.* Charlotte, Vermont: Williamson Publishing.

Jones, Sandy. (1979), *Learning for Little Kids: A Parent's Sourcebook for the Years 3 to 8.* Boston: Houghton Mifflin Company.

Kenda, Margaret and Williams, Phyllis. (1992), *Science Wizardry for Kids.* New York: Barron's.

Koenig, Larry. (2002), *Smart Discipline: Fast Lasting Solutions for Your Peace of Mind and Your Child's Self-Esteem.* New York: HarperResource (HarperCollins).

Krulik, Nancy. (2000), *Raise Your Child's Self-Esteem.* New York: Scholastic.

Lappe, Frances Moore. (1990), *Diet for a Small Planet.* New York: Ballantine Books.

Leman, Kevin. (1993), *Bringing Up Kids Without Tearing Them Down.* New York: Delacorte Press.

Lewis, Shari. (1960), *Fun with the Kids.* New York: Doubleday & Company, Inc.

Lima, Carolyn and Lima, John. (1998), *A to Zoo: Subject Access to Children's Picture Books.* New Providence, New Jersey: R.R. Bowker.

Lipson, Eden Ross. (1991), *The New York Times Parent's Guide to the Best Books for Children.* New York: Times Books (Random House).

Olen, Dale. (1996), *Self-Esteem for Children: A Parent's Gift That Lasts Forever.* Milwaukee, WI: JODA Communications.

Press, Judy. (1994), *Little Hands Art Book.* Charlotte, Vermont: Williamson Publishing.

Rosso, Julee. (1996), *Fresh Start: The Savvy Way to Cook, Eat, and Live!* New York: Crown Trade Paperbacks.

Saxion, Valerie. (2003), *Super Foods for Super Kids and Everyone Else Too!* Minneapolis, MN: Bronze Bow Publishing Inc.

Sher, Barbara. (1998), *Self-Esteem Games: 300 Fun Activities That Make Children Feel Good About Themselves.* New York: J. Wiley & Sons.

Teaching Tolerance Project. (1997), *Starting Small: Teaching Tolerance in Preschool and the Early Grades.* Montgomery, AL: Southern Poverty Law Center.

Taylor, Barbara. (1975), *When I Do, I Learn: A Guide to Creative Planning for Teachers and Parents of Preschool Children.* Provo, Utah: Brigham Young University Press.

Trelease, Jim. (2001), *The Read-Aloud Handbook (5th Edition).* New York: Penguin.

Wallace, Jeffrey Scott. (1994), *Discovering the Four Seasons: A Fun-Filled Guide to Spring, Summer, Autumn and Winter.* Elgin, IL: Lion Publishing.

READING TITLE INDEX

CRAFTING ACTIVITY INDEX

COOKING RECIPE INDEX

ABOUT THE AUTHOR

Vivian Kirkfield's love affair with children's picture books began over fifty years ago when she was given *THE LITTLE HOUSE* by Virginia Lee Burton as a present for her third birthday. Helping her mother turn the pages, a new and exciting world was revealed to her. As Vivian grew older and became involved with the care and education of young children, she came to regard the children's picture book as a valuable tool to be used, not only for entertainment and enjoyment, but also for helping children deal with the many issues they encounter in their early years.

After receiving a Bachelor of Arts Degree in Early Childhood Education, Vivian taught Kindergarten and Head Start while earning her Master of Science Degree. Taking a leave of absence to begin her own family, she decided to remain at home and implement her winning program with the children of local teachers in her own day care operation.

Throughout her career as an educator, Vivian has combined a positive attitude and loving manner with a unique program that uses structured activities and a daily picture book story. This successful program enabled the children in her care to gain the skills, knowledge and self-esteem that would facilitate their success in life. Her newsletter, *THE ESSENTIAL CHILD,* has been a valuable resource for parents and other caregivers of young children. **SHOW ME HOW! BUILD YOUR CHILD'S SELF-ESTEEM THROUGH READING, CRAFTING AND COOKING** is the first book in her new *POSITIVE PARENTAL PARTICIPATION* series. Vivian has also written a number of picture book stories that help toddlers learn their colors, numbers and ABC's.